THE CRYPTO HANDBOOK
A BEGINNER'S GUIDE TO UNDERSTANDING AND INVESTING IN CRYPTOCURRENCY

BOGDAN IVANOV

© **2023 Bogdan Ivanov - All rights reserved.**

This book is copyright protected. It is only for personal use. You cannot amend, distribute, sell, use, quote or paraphrase any part, or the content within this book, without the consent of the author or publisher.

Independently published |
Bogdan Ivanov
Württembergische Str. 18, 10707 Berlin, Germany

ISBN: 979-8391341727 Paperback

Disclaimer-Notice:

Please note the information contained within this document is for educational and entertainment purposes only. All effort has been executed to present accurate, up to date, reliable, complete information. No warranties of any kind are declared or implied. Readers acknowledge that the author is not engaged in the rendering of legal, financial, medical or professional advice. The content within this book has been derived from various sources. Please consult a licensed professional before attempting any techniques outlined in this book.

By reading this document, the reader agrees that under no circumstances is the author responsible for any losses, direct or indirect, that are incurred as a result of the use of the information contained within this document, including, but not limited to, errors, omissions, or inaccuracies.

I dedicate this book to my mom. Thank you for always wanting the best for me, for your unconditional love, and for endlessly worrying and continuing to worry about me.

—

Эту книгу я посвящаю своей маме. Спасибо тебе за то, что всегда желала мне лучшего, за твою бесконечную любовь, и за то, что бесконечно беспокоилась и продолжаешь беспокоиться обо мне.

CONTENTS

Introduction ix

1. OVERVIEW OF CRYPTOCURRENCIES 1
   How Cryptocurrencies Work 3
   Cryptography 3
   Blockchain Technology 3
   Decentralized Control 4
   Private Keys 5
   Cryptocurrency Wallets 6
   Miners 6
   Finite Supply 8
   Cryptocurrency Exchanges 8

2. THE FIRST CRYPTOCURRENCIES PROPOSALS
   IN THE 1980'S 11
   eCash—The First Cryptocurrency 12
   Other Early Cryptocurrencies 12
   The Launch of Bitcoin In 2009 13
   The Beginning Of The Crypto Market 14
   Ethereum and the introduction of ERC-20
   tokens. 15
   The Crypto Scam Era 17
   Types of Cryptocurrency Scams 17

3. HOW THE POPULARITY AND ACCEPTANCE
   OF BITCOIN SOARED 21
   The Rise Of Bitcoin 22
   The Structure Behind Bitcoin's Ideology 24
   Building A Smarter Coin 27
   Key Reasons For Cryptocurrency Acceptance
   And Popularity 29
   The Keys To Crypto Market Growth 32
   Top Impacting Factors 34

4. OPERATIONS OF CRYPTOCURRENCIES	39
Advantages Of Cryptocurrencies	41
5. DECENTRALIZED EXCHANGES	47
What Is a DEX (Decentralized Exchange)?	47
The Operation of Decentralized Exchanges	49
Order Book DEXs	50
Automated Market Makers (AMMs)	51
Evolution Of Decentralized Exchanges	52
What Are the Benefits of Decentralized Exchanges?	53
DEX Risks and Factors to Consider	55
6. DECENTRALIZED FINANCE	59
Overview Of Decentralized finance (DeFi)	60
What are smart contracts?	60
How was DeFi established?	61
The difficulties of centralized finance	61
How Risky is Investment in DeFi?	62
Prerequisites for Private Keys	64
Using DeFi	64
How Can Investors Profit From DeFi?	66
DeFi protocols and their operation	67
What challenges do DeFi projects face?	68
The Importance of DeFi	71
7. BLOCKCHAIN/CRYPTOCURRENCY WALLETS	73
Features of blockchain wallets	74
Blockchain Wallet Address	76
The creation of a blockchain wallet address	76
How a blockchain wallet works	79
Types Of Blockchain Wallets	80
Creation And Usage Of A Blockchain Wallet For Crypto Transaction	84
Functions Of A Blockchain Wallet	86
Benefits of using a cryptocurrency wallet	86

8. DETERMINING THE BEST CRYPTO WALLET
   FOR YOU   89
   Top Factors to Consider Before Choosing the
   Best Crypto Wallet   90
   Safeguarding Your Crypto Wallet   95

9. THE TOP CRYPTOCURRENCY WALLETS   101

10. GUIDE TO TRADING CRYPTOCURRENCIES   113
    Overview Of Cryptocurrency Trading   114
    Difference Between Investing and Trading   115
    Fundamental Analysis (FA)   116
    Technical Analysis (TA)   119
    On-chain Analysis   120

11. UNDERSTANDING THE CRYPTO MARKET   123
    Market Trend   124
    Market Cycle   125
    Chasing the Whale   126
    Psychological Cycles   127
    Basic Tools   128
    Support and Resistance   128
    Trendlines   129
    Round Number   129
    Moving Averages   130
    Chart Patterns   130

12. STRUCTURE AND STRATEGIES OF CRYPTO
    TRADING   133
    Structure of a Trade   133
    Trading Strategy   134
    Different Types of Trading Strategies   135
    Other Types Of Crypto Trading Strategies   138

13. HOW TO START TRADING
    CRYPTOCURRENCIES   143
    A Beginner's Guide To Cryptocurrency Trading   144
    Considerations For Trading Cryptocurrencies   145
    Other Things To Understand Before Trading
    Cryptocurrencies   149

14. BECOMING A SUCCESSFUL CRYPTO TRADER 153
   Profitability Of Crypto Trading 156
   Passive vs. Active Investing in Cryptocurrencies 157
   The Basics on How to Become a Crypto Trader 162
   What The Best Crypto Traders Have in Common 164
   Risks Involved In Trading Cryptocurrency 165

15. HOW TO TRADE CRYPTOCURRENCIES
   RESPONSIBLY 169
   Importance Of Planning 170
   Ethical Trading 171
   Tips To Help You Trade Crypto Responsibly 171

16. GROWING YOUR WEALTH WITH
   CRYPTOCURRENCIES 181

   Conclusion 189
   Bibliography 193
   About the Author 197

INTRODUCTION

Despite only being around for less than 10 years, cryptocurrencies have seen rapid growth and widespread adoption. Assets tied to cryptocurrencies have started to appear in the portfolios and trading methods of numerous hedge funds and asset managers. Similar efforts have been made by the academic community to study crypto trading and propose standards for it. This book aims to provide a thorough overview of various aspects related to cryptocurrencies and give the novice reader the foundation to trade, invest in, and grow his or her wealth with these new forms of digital assets.

I am certain we've all seen the rising number of financial institutions incorporating cryptocurrencies into their portfolios over the past several years. In just 10 short years, the world went from just hearing about peer-to-peer (P2P) transactions to a $1 trillion crypto market. But to understand the cryptocurrency phenomenon, it's important to first learn about its origin, purpose, and advantages over traditional fiat currencies. Although they share some characteristics with more

INTRODUCTION

conventional assets, they have a unique nature, and our understanding of how they behave as assets is constantly developing.

You've probably seen that cryptocurrencies (and the terminology associated with them) have generated a lot of discussion in the media, online forums, and perhaps even in casual conversations between colleagues, friends, and family members. Despite the excitement, many individuals still don't understand what these terms mean or what the implication of cryptocurrency is. A lot of high-profile websites and events are trying to educate everyone, but they wrap crypto in a cloud of complex terminology to sound authoritative and knowledgeable. I've decided to adopt a different approach and explain it simply and give you—the reader—context so you understand how using cryptocurrencies fits in the broader financial landscape.

Initially seen as havens for criminals and money launderers, cryptocurrencies have advanced significantly in terms of both technology and acceptance. The market capitalization of cryptocurrencies reached $2 trillion in 2020 and is projected **to hit $10 trillion during the next bull run**. According to reports, the technology that underpins cryptocurrencies has significant uses in industries as diverse as software development, agriculture, energy production, media, and healthcare.

Despite this, cryptocurrencies are still divisive. While some, like investor Marc Andreessen, refer to Bitcoin as "the future internet," others, including economist Paul Krugman and businessman Warren Buffet, term it "evil" and a "mirage." Every person who claims that cryptocurrencies are in a bubble is countered by someone who is adamant that they are the next step in democratizing finance. At their most basic, they are the latest fad in fintech, but at their most advanced, they represent a revolutionary technology that challenges the social, political, and economic foundations of society.

This book explains the advantages of cryptocurrencies, their complicated underlying technology, and how a digital form of money may be used as a storage of value and to grow wealth. It also looks at the key issues of crypto and, most importantly, how anyone can profit by investing in cryptocurrencies.

Let's get started.

ONE
OVERVIEW OF CRYPTOCURRENCIES

 If you don't believe it or don't get it, I don't have the time to try to convince you, sorry.

SATOSHI NAKAMOTO

Cryptocurrencies are digital assets that use cryptography as a form of encryption to ensure security. Although some newer cryptocurrencies also offer a set of rules or obligations for their holders—something I will address later—they are primarily used to buy and trade goods and services or as a form of speculation. Governments have remained split regarding recognizing cryptocurrencies as viable storage of wealth or form of currency. They are not recognized as legal cash and, unlike conventional currency, are not issued by a centralized body.

At this time, only a small number of "early adopters" in the business sector use cryptocurrencies, although this number increases daily. In terms of size, there are about 10 million users of Bitcoin globally, with about half using it as an investment. The benefits of cryptocurrencies are largely hypothetical for adopters. Therefore, widespread adoption won't happen unless there is a large, real-world advantage to utilizing a cryptocurrency and better standards and frameworks to regulate them.

Most cryptocurrencies operate similarly to Bitcoin, the original and most popular cryptocurrency. The value of cryptocurrencies is expressed in units, just like traditional currencies. For example, you can say, "I have 2.5 Bitcoins," which is equivalent to saying, "I have $2.50," something that was true 10 years ago. Of course, $1,000 invested in Bitcoin in 2010 was worth $287.5 million in 2020. Many cryptocurrencies produced gains of between 2,000% and 4,000% during the last bull market.

The onset of cryptocurrencies has produced a group of users who are comfortable with this asset class and its technology. But too many cryptocurrencies remain shrouded in mystery and are less than legit. A less-than-positive media campaign has managed to vilify cryptocurrency because of the independence it gives users. Unlike fiat and central currencies, crypto is un-governable and thus harder to track and control. On the other hand, a number of dangers and disadvantages, including illiquidity and value volatility, are associated with cryptocurrencies that don't apply to many fiat currencies.

A lot of countries have outright banned cryptocurrencies because they are commonly used to promote gray and black market transactions. With the notable exception of Bitcoin and a select few other coins, few serious financial professionals see most cryptocurrencies as acceptable for anything more than pure speculation, despite the fact that proponents pitch them as potentially lucrative alternative investments.

HOW CRYPTOCURRENCIES WORK

The smart contracts and source codes that support and secure cryptocurrencies are quite complicated. But even the average person can grasp the fundamental ideas and use cryptocurrencies responsibly. The values, security, and integrity of cryptocurrencies are governed by a number of objectives and functions.

CRYPTOGRAPHY

To protect their units of exchange, cryptocurrencies employ cryptographic protocols, or incredibly intricate code. These protocols are created by developers using cutting-edge mathematics and computer engineering principles, making it nearly impossible to crack them and thereby copy or counterfeit the protected assets. Additionally, these protocols conceal the identity of cryptocurrency users, making it challenging to link transactions and money flows to particular people or organizations.

BLOCKCHAIN TECHNOLOGY

The primary public ledger that keeps track of all previous transactions and activity and validates ownership of all units of a cryptocurrency is called the blockchain. A blockchain has a set length, contains a finite number of transactions, and grows over time. It contains the complete history of all transactions for a cryptocurrency to date.

Every node of the cryptocurrency's software network, or the network of decentralized server farms managed by computer-savvy individuals or organizations known as miners, continuously records and authenticates bitcoin transactions. It also stores identical copies of the blockchain for the purpose of avoiding unauthorized edits.

Technically, a bitcoin transaction isn't complete until it's uploaded to the blockchain, which typically happens in minutes. Once the process is complete, it usually cannot be undone. Unlike PayPal and credit cards, most cryptocurrencies don't have built-in chargeback or refund features. Some newer cryptocurrencies do offer basic refund functionality, but this is the exception, not the rule.

The transferred crypto is not available for use by either party during the interim period between the commencement and completion of the transaction. Instead, the sum is effectively kept in a form of escrow. The alteration of bitcoin code to enable the same currency units to be reproduced and distributed to numerous recipients, or double-spending, is thus prevented by the blockchain.

DECENTRALIZED CONTROL

The idea of decentralized control is ingrained in blockchain technology. This is where they differ from money backed and governed by central banks or other regulatory bodies. It is the actions of the blockchain's users and the smart contracts that determine the supply and value of cryptocurrencies.

The activities of miners, in particular, are essential to the stability and smooth operation of cryptocurrencies. I will go into detail about the role of miners later in the book, but it's important to know that miners are cryptocurrency users who use enormous amounts of computing power to record transactions on the blockchain. This way, they contribute to maintaining it and are rewarded with newly created cryptocurrency units and transaction fees paid by other users in return.

PRIVATE KEYS

Each cryptocurrency owner has a private key that confirms their identity and permits them to access, trade, and transact with their digital assets. Users can generate these private keys manually or with the aid of a random number generator. The format is that of a whole number that contains up to 78 digits. The holder cannot spend or convert their crypto without the key, making their holdings worthless until the key is found.

Lost private keys account for one of the ways Bitcoin is removed from circulation. Since Bitcoin owners need access to their private keys or recovery phrase to transfer their Bitcoin, anybody that loses access to these will also lose the ability to spend their funds.

Although it is a crucial security measure that prevents theft and illegal usage, this measure is also onerous. The analogy between losing your private key and burning a wad of cash in the garbage is that of digital assets. Although you can generate a new private key and begin acquiring cryptocurrency once more, you cannot get back the assets secured by your previous, lost key.

Smart cryptocurrency users are consequently maniacally careful of their private keys, frequently storing them on paper or in another physical form as well as in numerous digital locations that are typically not connected to the Internet for security reasons.

CRYPTOCURRENCY WALLETS

Users of cryptocurrencies have wallets with distinctive information proving they are the rightful owners of their assets. Wallets reduce the risk of theft for unusable bitcoin units, whereas private keys certify the legitimacy of a cryptocurrency transaction.

Cryptocurrency exchanges' usage of wallets makes them somewhat susceptible to hacking. As an illustration, the Japanese-based Mt. Gox Bitcoin exchange shut down and filed for bankruptcy a few years ago after hackers methodically stole more than $450 million in Bitcoin that had been traded on its systems. Wallets may be kept on a local hard drive, external storage hardware, or the cloud. No matter how a wallet is kept, it is extremely advisable to have at least one backup. Keep in mind that when you backup your wallet, you only copy the information about the bitcoin units that are currently in your possession.

MINERS

For bitcoin communities, miners act as record-keepers and proximate value arbitrators. Miners employ incredibly powerful computational resources, frequently found in private server farms operated by mining collectives made up of hundreds of individuals, to verify the accuracy, completeness, and security of the blockchains of different currencies.

The operation's size is comparable to the search for new prime numbers, which similarly necessitates a significant amount of processing power. By adding recent, previously unverified transactions that aren't present in any earlier blockchain copy, miners' work builds fresh copies of the blockchain on a regular basis, thereby concluding those transactions. Every addition is referred to as a "block." All transactions carried out since the last new copy of the blockchain was produced are collected in blocks.

The word "miners" refers to the fact that their labor essentially produces money in the form of fresh bitcoin units. Every fresh blockchain copy is really accompanied by a two-part financial reward: a fixed number of newly produced ("mined") cryptocurrency units and a variable number of existing units gathered from buyers' optional transaction fees, which are normally less than 1% of the transaction value.

For those with the funds to invest in power- and hardware-intensive mining operations, cryptocurrency mining used to be a potentially successful side industry. Since professional-grade mining equipment costs thousands of dollars, it is currently impractical for hobbyists to purchase it. There are many freelancing opportunities that offer better returns if your goal is to just complement your current income.

Although sellers are exempt from paying transaction fees, miners are still allowed to give fee-loaded transactions priority over fee-free ones when building new blocks, even if the fee-free ones arrived first in time. Because they receive their money more quickly, this offers sellers an incentive to charge transaction fees; hence, fees are frequently added to bitcoin transactions. Although it is theoretically feasible for previously unconfirmed transactions on a new blockchain copy to be completely fee-free, this nearly never occurs in practice.

Cryptocurrencies automatically adapt to the amount of computing power needed to make new blockchain copies according to instructions in their source code; copies get harder to make as mining power rises and simpler to make as it falls. The objective is to maintain a constant average gap between fresh blockchain productions at a predefined threshold. For instance, Bitcoin's is 10 minutes.

FINITE SUPPLY

Even if new cryptocurrency units are occasionally created through mining, the majority of cryptocurrencies are created with a limited supply as a crucial value guarantee. This often means that as time passes, miners earn less new units with every fresh block. Even though this has not yet occurred in practice and might not for some time, miners will eventually only be paid transaction fees for their work.

If current trends hold, experts estimate that the final Bitcoin will be mined sometime in the middle of the 22nd century, for example. This is not exactly in the near future. Cryptocurrencies are intrinsically deflationary because of their finite supply, making them more like gold and other precious metals, which also have restricted supplies, than fiat currencies, which central banks can theoretically print in endless quantities.

CRYPTOCURRENCY EXCHANGES

Many less popular cryptocurrencies can only be exchanged through private, peer-to-peer transfers, which makes them less liquid and makes it difficult to value them in comparison to other currencies—both crypto and fiat—because they are not widely used. More well-known cryptocurrencies, like Bitcoin and Ripple, are traded on specialized secondary exchanges that resemble forex markets for fiat money. (One instance of an exchange is the now-defunct Mt. Gox.) These platforms enable owners to trade their cryptocurrency holdings for other cryptocurrencies, including less well-known ones, as well as for significant fiat currencies, such as the U.S. Dollar and Euro.

They receive a tiny fee from each transaction's value in exchange for their services—often less than 1%. Importantly, cryptocurrencies have variable exchange rates with important world currencies like the U.S. Dollar, British Pound, European Euro, and Japanese Yen. This is because they can be converted into fiat money on specific online markets.

Exchanges for prominent cryptocurrencies help establish liquid markets and determine how much they are worth in relation to fiat money. On some cryptocurrency exchanges, you may even trade derivatives in cryptocurrencies, and you can use crypto indexes to follow large cryptocurrency portfolios.

Exchange pricing, however, can still be very erratic. For instance, following the demise of Mt. Gox, the price of Bitcoin in U.S. Dollars dropped by more than 50%, then soared almost tenfold in 2017 as the demand for cryptocurrencies skyrocketed. Additionally, cryptocurrency exchanges are a target for hackers and thieves like those who brought down Mt. Gox, as they are the most popular location for the theft of digital currencies.

TWO
THE FIRST CRYPTOCURRENCIES PROPOSALS IN THE 1980'S

 Cryptocurrency is such a powerful concept that it can almost overturn governments.

CHARLES LEE

When American cryptographer David Chaum published a conference paper in 1983 explaining an early type of anonymous cryptographic electronic money, the concept of cryptocurrencies first came to light. The idea was to create a kind of money that could be distributed anonymously and without the need for centralized organizations (i.e., banks). Based on his original concepts, Chaum created the proto-cryptocurrency Digicash in 1995. Before money could be delivered to a destination, it needed certain encryption keys and user software to withdraw money from a bank.

Nick Szabo created Bit Gold in 1998, which is frequently seen as a direct forerunner to Bitcoin. Participants had to devote computer resources to solving cryptographic challenges, and those that did so were rewarded. It creates something that closely resembles Bitcoin when combined with Chaum's work.

However, without the aid of a centralized authority, Szabo was unable to resolve the famed double-spending issue (digital data can be copied and pasted). As a result, it took another ten years before an unknown individual or group acting under the alias Satoshi Nakamoto launched the development of Bitcoin and other cryptocurrencies by disseminating a white paper titled "Bitcoin - A Peer-to-Peer Electronic Cash System."

ECASH—THE FIRST CRYPTOCURRENCY

American cryptographer David Chaum proposed an electronic payment system in 1983. He envisioned a token currency that could be safely and quietly transferred between people; the parallels to contemporary cryptocurrencies are startling.

Chaum created a "blinding formula" that is used to encrypt data transmitted between people. Thus, "Blinded Cash"—a form of payment that can be altered without leaving a trace—could be safely moved between people.

A few years later, Chaum launched DigiCash to implement his idea by developing the first electronic payment system based on cryptography, named eCash. Despite going out of business in 1998, DigiCash's theories, as well as some of its algorithms and encryption tools, had a significant impact on the creation of following digital currencies.

OTHER EARLY CRYPTOCURRENCIES

B-money is an "anonymous, distributed electronic cash system" that was proposed in 1998 by developer Wei Dai. Dai proposed two distinct protocols, one of which required an unjammable and synchronous broadcast channel. B-money was never successful in the end and had several differences from Bitcoin. However, it was also an attempt at a private, secure, and anonymous electronic payment system.

THE LAUNCH OF BITCOIN IN 2009

Bitcoin is the most well-known cryptocurrency and a type of digital and global payment mechanism. People that need to transmit money across borders without interference from banks or governments are becoming more and more interested in Bitcoin. However, due to its quick increase in value, some people find it challenging to decide how to use their Bitcoins.

The Bitcoin white paper, outlining the operation of the Bitcoin blockchain network, was released on October 31, 2008, by Satoshi Nakamoto. When Satoshi bought Bitcoin.org on August 18, 2008, they formally started working on the bitcoin project. Although it's not the focus of this book, it's important to note that blockchain technology, which at its most basic level is constructing immutable data structures, is essential to the existence of Bitcoin (and all other cryptocurrencies).

The development of Bitcoin was in progress. On January 3, 2009, Satoshi Nakamoto mined the first block of the Bitcoin network. In this first block, they included a headline from The Times, providing a permanent allusion to the economic circumstances—involving bank bailouts and a centralized financial system—that Bitcoin was in part a reaction against.

The Genesis Block is the current name for this initial block, which led to the mining of 50 bitcoins. During this time, as well as the first few months of its existence, bitcoin had essentially no value. In April 2010, six months after bitcoin first became tradable, one BTC was worth just under 14 cents. The cost rose to 36 cents by early November before leveling off at about 29 cents.

Hal Finney and Nakamoto traded Bitcoin for the first time on January 12, 2009. Not until a guy bought 10,000 Bitcoins for two pizzas delivered by Papa John's in February of the following year did anyone comprehend the potential value of this new technology. Now, the value of that deal would be millions of dollars.

THE BEGINNING OF THE CRYPTO MARKET

In the beginning of 2010, Bitcoin was the only cryptocurrency available. It cost only a few cents at the time. New digital currencies entered the market throughout the ensuing years, and their values fluctuated along with that of Bitcoin.

During this time of turbulence, many people lost hope in cryptocurrencies as an avenue for investing. However, cryptos started to experience exceptional growth starting in late 2017. Prior to falling later that month, the combined market capitalization of all cryptocurrencies had hit $820 billion in January 2018. The cryptocurrency market has grown consistently throughout, despite this crash.

After Bitcoin became the first cryptocurrency, ways to trade them had to be developed. The first cryptocurrency exchange, known as bitcoinmarket.com, debuted in March 2010, although it is now defunct. Mt.Gox also began operations in July of that year.

Between 2011 and 2013, Bitcoin was able to match the value of the US Dollar in February. This year saw the emergence of a few competing cryptocurrencies: The cryptocurrency market had 10 digital assets, including Litecoin, as of May 2013. XRP, yet another significant cryptocurrency asset, joined in August (Ripple).

The first hacks appeared as Bitcoin's worth soared. The first Mt.Gox breach occurred in June 2011; 2,000 BTC, worth about $30,000 at the time, were taken. At its height, Mt.Gox was the biggest cryptocurrency exchange, processing 70% of all Bitcoin transactions.

Unfortunately, Mt.Gox was the victim of the first significant cryptocurrency exchange hack in 2014 when 850,000 BTC were taken from it. The amount of BTC stolen is the largest in the history of the cryptocurrency, which was worth $460,000,000 at the time ($9.5 billion at the time of writing). After this unique event, the price of Bitcoin fell by 50% and did not return to its original value until late 2016. Since then, cryptocurrency exchange hacks have continued to occur, though rarely to the same extent as Mt.Gox.

ETHEREUM AND THE INTRODUCTION OF ERC-20 TOKENS.

The Ethereum network was launched on July 30th, 2015. In terms of market capitalization, it is currently the second-largest crypto asset. It introduced decentralized finance and smart contracts to the cryptocurrency world. These enable the Ethereum blockchain to support its own native currency, Ether, as well as a full ecosystem on its blockchain (ETH). Wei is another name for the lowest unit of Ether (0.000,000,000,000,000,001 ETH).

Tokens are digital currencies that rely on the blockchain of another digital asset rather than having their own dedicated blockchain. ERC-20 tokens are those that are used on the Ethereum network. In 2015, the first-ever ERC token was released. That was the Augur cryptocurrency asset. Since then, the Ethereum blockchain has seen the creation of a huge number of tokens. Due to the fact that there are presently more than 200,000 ERC tokens, a sizable cryptocurrency ecosystem is active on a single blockchain.

Since then, the cryptocurrency industry has continued to grow. In January 2018, prices for bitcoin reached a record high. Since then, many new crypto assets have entered the market, including EOS (July 2017), Tron (September 2017), and Cardano (October 2017). Over 2000 digital currencies are already available on the bitcoin market, which is continually growing.

In fact, it is easy to see how cryptocurrencies are gradually spreading over the world. The acceptance and use cases for cryptocurrencies are growing as a result of the expanding trend. Even the development of a Central Bank Digital Currency (CBDC) is underway today, and prominent corporations are investing in cryptocurrencies and blockchain to demonstrate their growing interest in these technologies. Those kinds of things will undoubtedly drive the market's rapid expansion. The popularity of crypto assets has also increased to the point where adoption has become more significant and prevalent. There are more and more Bitcoin ATMs, more businesses are accepting cryptocurrencies as payment, crypto assets are being utilized for fundraisers, and you can even use cryptocurrencies to tour the world!

This list is growing quickly, just like the prices of cryptocurrencies have recently. Do not forget that the price of Bitcoin was less than $1,000 three years ago.

THE CRYPTO SCAM ERA

The year of cryptocurrencies was 2017. The number of schemes and frauds aimed at cryptocurrency investors also increased as the value of Bitcoin and other digital money soared. Fraudulent initial Coin Offerings (ICOs) and phishing scams allowed thieves to steal millions of dollars from unwitting victims eager to cash in on the cryptocurrency frenzy.

TYPES OF CRYPTOCURRENCY SCAMS

Scams involving cryptocurrencies typically fall into one of two categories:

1. Efforts to gain access to a target's digital wallet or authentication information This means that con artists attempt to obtain information that will grant them access to a digital wallet or other kinds of sensitive data, such as security codes. This can occasionally even mean having access to actual hardware.

2. Sending cryptocurrency directly to a con artist as a result of impersonation, phony business or investment opportunities, or other nefarious methods.

Social Engineering Scams

In social engineering scams, scammers use psychological tricks and lies to get important information about user accounts. These scams trick victims into believing that they are interacting with a reputable organization, such as a reputable company, tech support, a member of the community, a coworker, or a friend. Scammers frequently use any strategy or length of time necessary to win over a potential victim's trust and convince them to divulge sensitive information or send money to the scammer's virtual wallet. So when one of these reliable connections asks for cryptocurrency for any reason, it's often a sign of a scam.

Romance Scams

Dating websites are frequently used by con artists to dupe their victims into thinking they are actually committed to a long-term relationship. Once trust has been established, the topic of rich cryptocurrency prospects and the eventual transfer of either money or account identification credentials frequently comes up in conversation. Cryptocurrency accounted for almost 20% of the reported losses from romance scams.

Imposter and Giveaway Scams

Scammers also attempt to assume the identities of well-known politicians, business leaders, or bitcoin influencers as they move down the sphere of influence. In what is known as a "giveaway scam," many con artists claim to match or multiply the cryptocurrency provided to them in order to attract the attention of potential targets. A sense of legitimacy and urgency may frequently be created by carefully designed messaging coming from what frequently appears to be a legitimate social media account. People may transfer money rapidly in the expectation of receiving an immediate return because of this fictitious "once-in-a-lifetime" chance.

Phishing Scams

In the bitcoin industry, phishing scams try to get information about online wallets. Private keys for crypto wallets, which are needed to access the wallet's money, are of particular interest to con artists. Their operating procedure is similar to that of several well-known frauds. They direct the recipients of an email to a specifically designed website where they must submit private key information. The bitcoin that is stored in those wallets can be stolen by hackers once they have obtained this information.

Blackmail and Extortion Scams

Email blackmail is another common social engineering technique scammers employ. In these emails, con artists threaten to reveal the user's past visits to adult or other illegal websites and demand cryptocurrencies or private keys in exchange for their cooperation. These kinds of situations reflect a criminal effort at extortion and have to be reported to a law enforcement organization like the FBI.

Investment or Business Opportunity Scams

If something seems too good to be true, it probably isn't true. This proverb applies to all types of investing, but it holds true for cryptocurrencies in particular. Numerous profit-seeking speculators visit dubious websites that promise guaranteed returns or other schemes requiring substantial investments in exchange for even larger assured returns. While money is readily flowing in, these false pledges frequently result in financial disaster when people try to withdraw their money and are unable to do so.

Cloud Mining Scams

Platforms will encourage small-scale purchasers and investors to commit money up front in order to guarantee a steady supply of mining power and rewards. These platforms do not genuinely possess the hash rate they claim to, and they will not pay out the benefits after your initial investment. Even though cloud mining is not always a scam, careful research on the platform must be done before investing.

THREE
HOW THE POPULARITY AND ACCEPTANCE OF BITCOIN SOARED

> *My hope for Bitcoin is that it can improve the efficiency of the information system that we call 'money.'*
>
> ELON MUSK

A new financial counterculture began when Nakamoto emailed Hal Finney 10 bitcoins on January 12, 2010. The value of the bitcoin was now insignificant. In essence, users rewarded one another with bitcoins for insightful forum posts. On May 22, 2010, the first "actual" transaction occurred. Laszlo Hanyecz paid 10,000 bitcoin, or roughly $30, for two pizzas. (10,000 bitcoins would be worth several millions of US Dollars today.)

For the most of its existence, bitcoin attracted support from three primary overlapping communities: the small group of early investors and real believers, the enthusiasts for blockchain technology, and the money-hungry speculators.

Another group has recently begun to emerge: traditional, stuffy financial types.

Instead of a central bank, bitcoin's original design and Nakamoto's whitepaper suggested skepticism toward conventional financial institutions. This made bitcoin money with a philosophy. Yet Nakamoto disappeared. The system, which was designed to function without trust, started to have trust problems as the digital currency gained popularity. The financial system that bitcoin was designed to replace has gained another investment vehicle as its price has increased. Ten years later, Bitcoin is still a component of the system it was designed to replace.

THE RISE OF BITCOIN

One was developed in 2008, during the height of the banking crisis, by a group of anarchists, libertarians, and other disgruntled tech-savvy true believers. (Other experiments with digital currency existed, but none of them really took off.) A domain for "bitcoin" was registered in August 2008, and on Halloween of that same year, a paper outlining a decentralized, trustless system for electronic transactions was published. An entirely peer-to-peer version of electronic cash would enable internet payments to be transmitted directly from one party to another without going through a financial institution, according to the opening paragraph of the original Satoshi Nakamoto white paper.

The ideology of bitcoin is clearly influenced by the banking crisis. To start, there is a particular mistrust of financial institutions. In addition to other betrayals of trust that occurred during the financial crisis, a money market fund under the name of Reserve Primary Fund breached the law. You would have received 97 cents back on a $1 investment. This was due to the money market fund's investment in the recently bankrupt banking institution Lehman Brothers.

As of September 2008, $3 trillion had been put into money market funds, which at the time were thought to be as secure as a real savings account, according to USA Today. They did, however, have higher rates of return because they are less secure than savings accounts, as investors discovered to their shock and dismay. (Subsequently, money market fund regulations were altered.)

It became evident how closely connected banks were when Lehman's bankruptcy extended to other financial markets. One response to this is to tighten financial laws, make adjustments to the system, and then let it continue to function, hopefully in a more stable fashion. Making a new system without these specific hazards is another option. Suddenly, many people had the desire to treat bitcoin seriously.

Bitcoin serves as a reminder of how peculiar money is at its core. Money isn't "real" in the same sense that a tree is. It is a creation of humans, a value token that facilitates exchange. But it's true enough; for it, people fight and die; for lack of it, empires crumble; as for myself, if I didn't use it to pay my rent, I'd be homeless. If enough people believe in it, money is real, much like Tinkerbell in Peter Pan. And a lot of individuals were searching for alternatives to the mainstream banking system in 2009 because it had disastrously failed. Money is at the center of banking, as most people understand it. But without the bankers, what does money look like? Bitcoin emerged as the most viable response to society's general concerns about the financial system among all the prior attempts at internet-based currency, and there were many.

THE STRUCTURE BEHIND BITCOIN'S IDEOLOGY

The way Bitcoin is set up makes its ideology clear. A peer-to-peer financial network is a notion that is reminiscent of classic Silicon Valley disruption. Sending money to a third party, such as a bank or Western Union, is free of charge. But the original ideology goes much further than that: if you think that the state is just a tool for committing violence, you can also think that fiat money, like the dollar, is a coercive state monopoly. Bitcoin challenges that monopoly and acts in part as a method of government-based resentment.

This idea is implied even in the word "mine," as many investors consider bitcoin to be a commodity similar to gold. (Let's bow before the gold standard and continue.) Additionally, bitcoin is a limited resource; according to the existing system, there can only be 21 million bitcoin worldwide. Already mined are more than 17 million. The remaining portion will be made available at a consistent mining pace, which has slowed as more of the resources have been created. No president or central bank can speed up the economy or raise inflation to further their own political goals.

The other key technology for dodging banking institutions —and the state—is the distributed ledger. Anyone can access the public parts of the "blockchain," a ledger of all transactions made over time. No institution, at least in theory, is required to ensure trustworthy transactions. If you can keep your wallet anonymous, they don't even need to know who you are.

However, as the past ten years have shown, eliminating

trust from one area of the financial system causes trust issues to arise in other areas, which is how the counterculture came into being. You had to persuade other people that their investment in bitcoin was good in order for it to be profitable. Communities for bitcoin have emerged on websites like Reddit and IRC.

The most significant community for early bitcoin, though, was the dark web marketplace Silk Road. Founded by Dread Pirate Roberts, who would later be revealed as Ross Ulbricht, the promise of Silk Road was also essentially libertarian. The idea was that anything could be traded, regardless of whether the state viewed it as legal. The trade was dominated by marijuana, fake IDs, benzos, and other prescription drugs that were all facilitated by bitcoin. When the Silk Road was seized by the US government in 2013, that seizure included 144,336 bitcoins that belonged to Ulbricht.

The shutdown of Silk Road marked the beginning of bitcoin's end. Untangling financial institutions from money may have been the turning point when it became apparent that neither a more trustworthy environment nor governmental protection were guaranteed by doing so. Mt. Gox's insolvency would make bitcoin's trust issues even worse.

Mt. Gox ("Magic: The Gathering Online eXchange") didn't start out as a bitcoin exchange, but it did so in early 2010. Bank transfers were accepted for buying and selling bitcoins on Mt. Gox, which was founded by Jed McCaleb and sold to Mark Karpelès in 2011. According to Adrianne Jeffries for The Verge, the early years of Mt. Gox showed that using digital currency came with new hazards, including "hacks, outages, a run-in with the US government, and a $75 million lawsuit."

After customers complained that they couldn't withdraw

their bitcoin, Mt. Gox declared bankruptcy in 2014. As of February 2014, Mt. Gox was thought to be in charge of trading 70% of all bitcoins ever moved; therefore, its bankruptcy may have been disastrous. Behind the scenes, according to Jeffries, "Karpelès had learned that a perpetrator had been stealthily taking all of Mt. Gox's bitcoins without being seen." In February 2014, the business declared bankruptcy, stating obligations of $64 million. The rise in the price of bitcoin in the years that followed allowed at least some of the creditors to cash out at rates from 2014, but that wasn't the actual issue. Bitcoin was supposed to prevent your money from being held hostage by a bankrupt bank, yet that's exactly what had happened.

The experience of trading bitcoin is made simpler by Mt. Gox and the other exchanges, which essentially act as the bitcoin equivalent of commodities exchanges. They make it possible for users to buy and sell cryptocurrencies, as well as convert fiat currency (state-issued money, such as dollars) into cryptocurrency and set the price for bitcoin and other cryptocurrencies. They brought new kinds of security threats along with them, and their existence made it simpler for regular people to start using bitcoin. Some of the early Mt. Gox issues afflicted later exchanges like Coinbase, suggesting that digital currency had fresh issues that paper-based currency did not.

While you could break into my house and take the $40 that sits next to my laptop, doing so would take a lot of time and yield little benefit. However, learning how to hack the exchanges may result in tens of millions of cash from one incident.

Although conventional banks and exchanges are not immune to hacking, they invest heavily in making themselves more difficult targets. However, according to John Sedunov, an assistant professor of finance at Villanova University, bitcoin exchanges "may not have had the funds on hand, time, or even the technical competence to scale up security features fast enough to ward off possible attackers."

BUILDING A SMARTER COIN

Even as the Silk Road was shut down and Mt. Gox went bankrupt, bitcoin kept gaining popularity. According to Cointelegraph, Microsoft started taking bitcoin payments around the end of 2014. The Economist featured a cover story about bitcoin in 2015. Other cryptocurrencies, like Ethereum, which are also based on the blockchain, started to appear during this time. Ethereum was launched in 2014 with an initial coin offering (ICO) that raised $18 million.

Another significant movement in the community began with Ethereum when the focus shifted from bitcoin itself to blockchain technology. Ethereum allows users to create applications and earn money from their efforts via the blockchain. The "smart contract" is the most popular application. (Even though this technology claims to be able to replace lawyers, once lawyers become involved, it is very difficult to persuade them to back out. Just a thought!) To illustrate how to create a smart contract, let's pretend that you and I have agreed that I will write you a history of bitcoin in exchange for you sending me $10 on my birthday this year. Either through a legally binding contract involving attorneys, notaries, and other professionals, or through Ethereum.

In the latter scenario, you escrow $10 worth of smart coins, which are released to me once the contract's conditions are satisfied. The coins are returned to you if I don't adhere to the terms of our agreement.

While Ethereum was the most significant of these firms, many other ICOs also emerged, including NXT Neo, Spectrecoin, Stratis, and EOS, which were frequently connected to particular businesses and goods. As more countries recognized these new cryptocurrencies as taxable, potentially regulated investment instruments, the enlarged world of blockchain technology—a phrase on which no one can agree—took shape. The US Securities and Exchange Commission, also known as "the money cops," said in 2017 that certain financing transactions for virtual currencies will be treated as securities, and it then proceeded to launch lawsuits against numerous shady coin projects for breaking securities laws.

Depending on your perspective, this may either validate cryptocurrencies ("it's so real that the government is deciding to regulate it as an investment vehicle!") or it could represent a breach of the original government-free promise upon which the Nakamoto entity founded bitcoin. But over time, the initial bitcoin believers' group had largely faded away.

Bitcoin's price increased by more than 1,000% in 2017, which may have contributed to the individuals who, you know, make money professionally having such a keen interest in it. (Later, a University of Texas finance professor hypothesized that market manipulation was responsible for half of this surge.) The price of bitcoin reached a record high of $20,000 on December 17th, 2017. Even though, by August 2018, a DEA agent informed Bloomberg that the bulk of bitcoin transactions were by speculators rather than the black market types that predominated bitcoin during the Silk Road days, cryptocurrency-related crime increased as well.

For those speculators, 2018 was particularly difficult as bitcoin dropped by 80% from its peak in 2017. The majority of consumers lost interest as its price dropped, while finance specialists, who can profit when an asset's value rises or falls, retained their attention.

The unexpected success of bitcoin outside of the banking sector has a price. Since so many individuals are mining bitcoin, the price of the powerful chips needed by researchers has increased, making it more challenging for, among others, astronomers to carry out their work. Climate hawks are concerned because bitcoin mining uses a lot of energy and emits a lot of emissions.

Despite numerous attempts, nobody has managed to figure out who Satoshi Nakamoto was or is. Although there have been many challengers, no one has yet offered the undeniable evidence: trading Nakamoto's bitcoin. The banking system's confidence issue appears to be over. But the institutional investors and banks that the system was intended to obviate may very well be the biggest beneficiaries of the new bitcoin era.

KEY REASONS FOR CRYPTOCURRENCY ACCEPTANCE AND POPULARITY

In 2022, cryptocurrency still seems like a good long-term investment option. Now that the year is drawing to a close, significant growth drivers have emerged, including the enormous market capitalization, the introduction of new and reliable firms into the crypto-space, and, most crucially, the real-world potential dependent on the fundamental blockchain technology.

But are these the only elements contributing to cryptocurrency's widespread acceptance? Not by a long shot, at least. Although the financial advantages of crypto are taken into consideration by its rising popularity, that is only the beginning. There must be additional reasons for this extraordinary surge in crypto acceptance, other than the fact that investors are pouring money into top crypto exchanges like CoinSwitch Kuber.

The Subjective Nature of Virtual Money

Cryptocurrency represents a positive shift for individuals who think of money as having objective qualities. Despite price increases, the most well-known cryptocurrencies, such as Bitcoin and Ethereum, have demonstrated remarkable worth, encouraging investors to enter this market from a broader perspective. Simply defined, the underlying crypto technology, or the blockchain-specific public ledger, has the potential to disrupt the current system of traditional payments. While this is one of the main factors contributing to crypto's widespread acceptability, there are five other important players who support this new type of currency even more.

Benefits to Merchants and Consumers

Cryptocurrency is currently a popular choice in the retail industry, benefiting from P2P payments and safe transactions. Due to the transactional safety in place, major businesses are allowing customers to pay with Bitcoins and even Altcoins despite the price fluctuation. Consumers will soon have access to innovative crypto-related services, thus the adoption is only anticipated to grow from here.

Change in the Existing Financial Mindset

Despite the fact that individuals still rely on banks, there has been turbulence around dealing with intermediation.

Unless you desire to make purchases, banks are in charge of and store your money. By eliminating middlemen that manage your hard-earned money, cryptocurrencies are gradually increasing the space's autonomy. Although this idea is still in its infancy, it has a great deal of unmistakable potential.

A Haven for Tech Developers

Professional developers are consistently making improvements to the crypto mining industry while planning newer approaches to reduce the process' energy consumption over time. In addition, new cryptocurrency players emerge every day with faster transactional rates, superior software development setups, and the capacity to produce blocks more quickly.

Surge in Investment

It's essential to reiterate the faith that individuals have in the cryptocurrency market, particularly when it comes to making large investments and holding positions for a long period of time. However, you should be aware that customers aren't paying for a specific business or standard value, but also for the intrinsic value of the presently available technology.

Relaxed Regulations

Do not allow China's strict position on cryptocurrencies to serve as a general guide for international regulations. Despite these strange anomalies, the entire worldwide system appears to be fairly upbeat, with El Salvador becoming the first nation to recognize Bitcoin as legal cash. This and other encouraging occurrences have helped crypto stand out in a market that has historically been quite inhospitable to new players.

Cryptocurrencies and the Range of Available Options

Money is simply money! While this is true for fiat currencies, crypto players are committed to providing a wide variety of options that are supported by cutting-edge technology.

Without prejudice or relative impacts, the underlying technology connected to a certain crypto player decides its worth over time. For instance, the sharp increase in the price of Ether, the relevant cryptocurrency, is due to Ethereum, a creative blockchain platform with a preference for smart contracts.

Cryptocurrencies for Institutional Players

The interest that institutional players have exhibited in cryptocurrencies must be one of the main factors driving its widespread adoption. People began to trust the rise as prices broke through many resistance zones and achieved new highs, which fueled more price growth and increased acceptability.

Still Onboard with the Sentimental Play

Even though there are some places where people trust cryptocurrencies, the market is still vulnerable to manipulation and emotive decisions. However, in 2022, major participants had figured out how to survive brief storms and only react gradually to good news, mirroring the more sustainable stock market. The fact that Bitcoin reached its ATH (all-time high) after Tesla announced a $1.5 billion investment in the same, or about 8% of the company's cash holdings, attests to this.

THE KEYS TO CRYPTO MARKET GROWTH

Market activity for cryptocurrencies has considerably grown. The interest in these currencies seems to have been more speculative—buying cryptocurrencies in an effort to earn a profit—than connected to their potential application as an innovative and distinctive payment mechanism. In connection with this, the values of various cryptocurrencies have experienced considerable volatility. For instance, Bitcoin's price rose from around US$30,000 in the middle of 2021 to almost US$70,000 in the end of 2021 before dropping to about US$35,000 in the beginning of 2022. Ether and other competing cryptocurrencies have seen comparable volatility. Due to the unprecedented interest in cryptocurrencies, more processing power is being employed to crack the intricate encryption that many of these systems use to keep them safe from being hacked. There is doubt over whether cryptocurrencies will ever completely replace more established payment methods or national currencies, despite the rise in interest in them.

The size of the worldwide cryptocurrency market, which was estimated to be worth $1.49 billion in 2020, is expected to increase to $4.94 billion by 2030, with a CAGR of 12.8% between 2021 and 2030. Virtual currency is another name for cryptocurrency. It is a sort of money that solely exists digitally and lacks a central issuing or governing body. Blockchain technology is used to verify the transactions. Blockchain is a decentralized technology that tracks and manages transactions across numerous computers. Additionally, it is a peer-to-peer system that enables users to send and receive payments from anywhere in the world and does not rely on banks to authenticate the transactions.

The main drivers of the expansion of the global cryptocurrency industry are the rising need for remittances in developing nations, the rise in demand for operational efficiency and transparency in financial payment systems, the improvement of data security, and the market cap. Additionally, the development of the cryptocurrency business is hampered by high implementation costs and little consumer knowledge of cryptocurrencies in emerging countries. A profitable possibility for market expansion is also anticipated due to the rise in demand for cryptocurrencies among banks and other financial institutions as well as the untapped potential of emerging nations.

Due to the increased need for software performance upgrades and solutions to make financial transactions more efficient, the hardware sector gained a significant portion of the cryptocurrency market. During the projected time frame for the cryptocurrency market, however, the software segment is expected to grow the fastest. This is because software makes it easier to handle the huge amount of data that is being created, which helps people get better insights and make better decisions.

Asia-Pacific dominated the cryptocurrency market by region in 2020, and it is anticipated that it will continue to do so throughout the forecast period. Because there are more Bitcoin exchanges popping up around Asia, the cryptocurrency market is becoming more mature and competitive. As the government promotes the use of Bitcoin technology to improve transparency and combat fraud in its financial sector, Chinese banks are employing blockchain expertise. The bitcoin market in the area is growing as a result of these causes.

TOP IMPACTING FACTORS

Increasing Demand for Payment System Transparency

Due to increased data transparency and independence across payments in banks, financial services, insurance, and several other business sectors, the cryptocurrency market is anticipated to experience promising growth in the years to come. The usage of cryptocurrency in the banking sector offers a number of advantages, including transparent payment sending and receipting as well as the secure storage of customer-specific information for future use.

Consider PayPal, an American business that participates in online payment systems. On October 21, 2020, it announced its entry into the cryptocurrency market and that users would be able to purchase and sell Bitcoin and other virtual currencies using their PayPal accounts. Additionally, on February 10, 2021, Mastercard introduced the first CBDC-linked card in the world in collaboration with Island Pay. Thus, a lot of these advancements among the key players fuel market expansion.

Furthermore, it is anticipated that cutting-edge blockchain distributed technology protocols would eliminate the requirement for specific organizational solutions and permit various parties to share payments transparently throughout the business. Such technologies increase supply chain transparency, assisting in the eradication of environmental crimes among other offenses. This encourages future cryptocurrency adoption.

Untapped Economic Potential in Emerging Markets

By facilitating greater access to finance and financial services, developing economies present enormous prospects for cryptocurrency to grow its operations. The most well-known of these cryptocurrencies, Bitcoin, has already allowed a lot of people and businesses to grow and thrive by serving as their main source of revenue. Cryptocurrencies have a huge potential to meet these needs as the economy gradually changes to accommodate them.

In emerging countries, changing demographics, rising consumerism, and receptivity to new technologies like IoT,

Blockchain, and others offer attractive potential for cryptocurrencies. Nigeria is the top nation for adopting Bitcoin and other cryptocurrencies, according to Oxford Business Group, because the country uses them to transmit remittances.

Bitcoin transactions were also allowed by the Philippine central bank. This results in the nation becoming one of the biggest bitcoin adopters in the world. In addition, the increased adoption of smartphones in Latin America and Africa allows mobile payment service providers to provide advanced services on mobile devices. This is viewed as a significant opportunity for the market's expansion.

How The Growing Use of Digital Currencies Will Impact the Crypto Market

The market is anticipated to grow in the coming years as a result of the acceptance of virtual or digital currencies like Bitcoins, Litecoins, Ethers, and many more. People in sophisticated nations are more inclined to use the simple and adaptable transactional technique that digital currency provides. The central bank decided to promote digital currency as a result of virtual currency's appeal as a means of exchange. For the digital currency programs across many industrialized countries, the central bank has patented Central Bank Digital Currency (CBDC) activity provisions.

For instance, the toolkit is being used in the CBDC evaluation process by the Bank of Thailand and the Central Bank of Uruguay, and the People's Bank of China and the Eastern Caribbean Central Bank both endorse CBDC's decision to use digital cash as a form of exchange. Digital currency is being offered by a number of businesses, including Facebook (now known as Meta). For instance, Facebook introduced a virtual currency called Libra in June 2019. Customers will be able to use Libra to make purchases, send money to others, and cash it out at grocery stores or online. Businesses can gain from shifting digital currency prices and fortify their digital assets.

Demand for the virtual currency is driven by a focus on combating the financial crisis and regional instability. Financial catastrophe is a significant problem that affects traditional banking and the financial industry. The economy is hampered by financial uncertainty since the value of the currency has declined. For instance, the 2008 Lehman Brothers crisis, which had an impact on the country's economy, was a huge issue for India's ICICI Bank. The financial crisis has had little impact on Bitcoin or other cryptocurrencies because of their uniformly balanced value. In regions with unstable economic systems, cryptocurrencies are a better option in terms of financial uncertainty, and this is increasingly a key market driving element.

The market for cryptocurrencies will experience exponential demand as Bitcoin adoption rises. One of the most widely used and well-known forms of digital currency is Bitcoin. Growing investor interest, increased visibility, and favorable rules are all contributing to the market's expansion. The market value of digital cash is also rising as a result of its maturing Bitcoin cash value and the ability to pay rewards for transactions. People's preference for digital money is evident in developing nations like Japan, the U.S., Europe, and many others, which is anticipated to facilitate the growth of the cryptocurrency sector in the approaching years.

FOUR
OPERATIONS OF CRYPTOCURRENCIES

> *Cryptocurrency currencies take the concept of money, and they take it native into computers, where everything is settled with computers and doesn't require external institutions or trusted third parties to validate things.*
>
> NAVAL RAVIKANT

Blockchain technology is what cryptocurrency relies on, but what precisely is a blockchain? The meaning and importance of the phrase are frequently muddled because it has become so widely used. Simply put, a blockchain is a computerized transactional ledger. A network of computer systems houses this ledger (or database). The ledger is controlled by multiple systems, and a decentralized network of computers maintains the blockchain and authenticates its transactions.

Blockchain technology is said to enhance security, trust, and transparency of data being shared across a network, according to its proponents. Blockchain critics claim that it can be inconvenient, expensive, ineffective, and energy-intensive.

If a digital asset's underlying blockchain is strong and useful, rational crypto investors will purchase it. Blockchain is the technology that underpins all cryptocurrencies, so cryptocurrency investors are placing bets on its robustness and allure whether they are aware of it or not.

Transactions involving cryptocurrencies are permanently recorded on the underlying blockchain. Blocks, which are collections of transactions that are added to the "chain," authenticate the legitimacy of the transactions and keep the network operational. The public shared ledger contains a record of every batch of transactions. Anyone may access the major blockchains, including Bitcoin (BTC) and Ethereum (ETH), and view the transactions that are being done there.

But why do individuals invest in computational resources to verify blockchain transactions? The correct response is that they receive payment in the underlying cryptocurrency. A proof-of-work (PoW) mechanism is the name of this incentive-based approach. Miners are the machines "working" to "verify" the legitimacy of blockchain transactions. The newly created cryptocurrency assets are given to miners in exchange for their energy.

Cryptocurrency investors don't keep their money in conventional bank accounts. They have digital addresses instead. The long strings of numbers and letters that make up these addresses are the private and public keys that allow cryptocurrency users to send and receive money. Cryptocurrency can only be unlocked and sent using private keys. Public keys are made available to the general public and allow the owner to accept cryptocurrency from any sender.

It is fair to say that Bitcoin has altered the status quo; nothing quite like it has ever existed before, and it has given rise to completely new technologies, platforms for investment, and ways of thinking about money. Electronic communications containing transaction instructions are delivered to the entire network during cryptocurrency transactions. The instructions include details like the parties' electronic addresses, the amount of money to be swapped, and a time stamp.

Let's say Andrew wishes to send Lisa one bitcoin unit. In order to begin the transaction, Andrew sends a network-wide electronic message containing her instructions. One of several transactions that have recently been sent is Andrew's. The transaction is waiting to be combined with other recent transactions into a block because the system is not immediate (which is just a group of the most recent transactions). To add the new block of transactions to the blockchain, miners compete to crack a cryptographic code created from the information within the block.

The network's other users verify the answer when a miner has successfully cracked the code, and they agree that it is correct. The blockchain is updated to include the fresh block of transactions, and Andrew's transaction is approved. Users can be guaranteed that their transaction has been successful by waiting for six blocks of transactions to be processed; therefore, this confirmation is not quick.

ADVANTAGES OF CRYPTOCURRENCIES

1. Self-governed and managed: Any currency's maintenance and governance are important for its growth. Developers/miners store cryptocurrency transactions on their hardware in exchange for a charge known as a transaction fee. Since they obtained it, the miners have kept transaction records accurate and up to date, maintaining the decentralized nature of the records and the integrity of the coin.

2. Decentralized: The fact that cryptocurrencies are largely decentralized is a major pro. Many cryptocurrencies are controlled by the people who create them, by those who own a large portion of them, or by businesses that create them before they are made available on the market. Contrary to fiat currencies, which are controlled by the government, cryptocurrencies are kept stable and secure by the decentralization, which helps keep the currency monopoly free and in check. As a result, no organization can decide the flow and, consequently, the value of the coin.

3. Currency exchanges are smooth: A variety of currencies, including the US dollar, European euro, British pound, Indian rupee, and Japanese yen, can be used to purchase cryptocurrencies. By trading cryptocurrencies across different wallets and paying low transaction fees, a variety of cryptocurrency exchanges and wallets facilitate currency conversion.

4. Simple fund transfers: Cryptocurrencies have consistently maintained their position as the best option for transactions. Cryptocurrencies enable instantaneous domestic and international transactions. It will be because there are only a few hurdles to overcome and the verification takes little time to complete.

5. Accessibility: Cryptocurrency can be used by anyone. An internet connection and a computer or smartphone are all you need. Comparing the process of creating an account at a conventional financial institution to that of setting up a bitcoin wallet, the latter is incredibly quick. There is no ID checking. There isn't a credit or background check.

With the use of cryptocurrency, people who lack bank accounts can access financial services directly. A person may be unable or reluctant to open a standard bank account for a variety of reasons. People who don't use traditional banking services may be able to send money to loved ones or conduct online transactions with ease by using cryptocurrencies.

6. Security: No one can sign transactions or access your funds unless they have access to the private key for your crypto wallet. However, there is also no way to get your money back if you misplace your private key.

Additionally, due to the design of the blockchain system and the distributed computer network that verifies transactions, transactions are secure. The network gets safer as more processing power is added to it. Before the rest of the network can certify the accuracy of the ledger, any attack on the network and any effort to manipulate the blockchain would need enough computer power to confirm numerous blocks. Such an assault is unaffordable for well-known blockchains like Bitcoin (CRYPTO:BTC) or Ethereum (CRYPTO:ETH). Cryptocurrency account hacks frequently result from lax security at a centralized exchange. It's safer to retain your cryptocurrency assets in your own wallet.

7. Privacy: You can keep some level of privacy when using cryptocurrencies because you don't need to sign up for an account at a financial institution. Pseudonymous transactions mean that while your wallet address serves as a unique identifier on the blockchain, it does not contain any personal data about you.

In many situations, having this much seclusion may be

advantageous (both innocent and illicit). However, once a wallet address is associated with an identity, the entire transaction history becomes visible. To increase the privacy of cryptocurrencies, there are numerous approaches to further hide transactions, as well as a number of privacy-focused coins.

8. Transparency: On the widely used blockchain ledger, all cryptocurrency transactions take place. Anyone can use tools to look up transaction information, including the where, when, and quantity of cryptocurrency sent from a wallet address. Also visible to anyone is the amount of cryptocurrency kept in a wallet.

Transparency to this extent can lessen fraudulent transactions. A person can demonstrate that they sent money and that it was received, or that they have the necessary finances to complete a transaction.

9. Speed of transaction: There aren't many ways to transfer money or assets from one account to another more quickly than you can with cryptocurrencies if you want to send money to someone in the United States. In U.S. financial institutions, the majority of transactions are settled within three to five days. Typically, a wire transfer takes at least 24 hours. In three days, stock trades are settled.

However, one benefit of bitcoin transactions is that they can be completed quickly. The funds are ready for usage after the network has confirmed the block containing your transaction.

10. Fees for transactions: Sending money across borders is one of the most common uses of cryptocurrencies. The transaction fees that a user must pay are eliminated or reduced to a small level with the use of cryptocurrencies. By not having to fulfill the requirement for third parties to validate a transaction, such as VISA or PayPal, it eliminates the need to pay any additional transaction costs.

Compared to other financial services, cryptocurrency transactions are comparatively inexpensive. For instance, a domestic wire transfer typically costs $25 to $30. Even more money can be spent when sending money abroad.

Transactions using cryptocurrencies are typically cheaper. You should be aware that the blockchain's demand may push up transaction costs. Even on the busiest blockchains, median transaction fees are still less than wire transfer expenses.

11. Diversification: Compared to conventional financial assets like equities and bonds, cryptocurrencies can provide investors with diversification. Although there is no historical data on how the cryptocurrency markets have performed in terms of equities or bonds, so far the values don't seem to be associated with those of other markets. They could be an excellent source for portfolio diversity because of this.

You can provide more consistent returns by mixing assets with low price correlation. Your crypto asset may increase if your stock portfolio decreases, and vice versa. Still, if your asset allocation is too heavily skewed toward cryptocurrencies, it may wind up making your entire portfolio more volatile.

12. Protection from inflation: Many believe that cryptocurrencies like Bitcoin and others can protect against inflation. The total amount of bitcoin coins that will ever be produced has a hard cap. Therefore, the price of Bitcoin should rise when the money supply expands faster than the amount of bitcoin does. There are several additional cryptocurrencies that use measures to limit supply and can serve as an inflation hedge.

The value of various currencies has fallen over time due to

inflation. Almost all cryptocurrencies are introduced with a fixed amount at the time of their inception. There are only 21 million bitcoins that have been released worldwide, according to the ASCII computer file, which lists the quantity of each coin. As a result, as demand rises, its value will rise as well, helping to keep the market stable and, in the long run, preventing inflation.

FIVE
DECENTRALIZED EXCHANGES

> *At their core, cryptocurrencies are built around the principle of a universal, inviolable ledger, one that is made fully public and is constantly being verified by these high-powered computers, each essentially acting independently of the others.*
>
> PAUL VIGNA

WHAT IS A DEX (DECENTRALIZED EXCHANGE)?

Users can trade cryptocurrencies in a non-custodial setting on a decentralized exchange (DEX), which is a peer-to-peer marketplace that eliminates the need for a middleman to handle the transfer and custody of funds. DEXs use blockchain-based smart contracts to replace traditional intermediaries, such as banks, brokers, payment processors, and other organizations, to enable the exchange of assets.

DEXs provide complete transparency into the movement of funds and the processes supporting exchange, in contrast to typical financial transactions, which are opaque and carried out through middlemen that provide very little insight into their actions. DEXs also lessen counterparty risk and can lessen systemic centralization problems in the bitcoin ecosystem because user money doesn't transit via a third party's cryptocurrency wallet during trading.

A key component of the cryptocurrency ecosystem, DEXs enable peer-to-peer exchange of digital assets between users without the involvement of middlemen. Due to their ability to supply new currencies with quick liquidity, their easy onboarding process, and the democratized access to trade and liquidity provision that they offer, DEXs have seen an increase in use over the past few years.

It is unclear whether the majority of trading activity will move to DEXs and whether the present DEX designs will sustain institutional acceptance and long-term growth. However, DEXs are anticipated to continue to see advancements in transaction scalability, smart contract security, governance infrastructure, and user experience. They are expected to remain an essential component of the cryptocurrency ecosystem.

Due to their permissionless composability, DEXs are a key "money LEGO" upon which more complex financial products can be built. DEXs are a cornerstone of decentralized finance (DeFi). This chapter discusses the many kinds of decentralized exchanges, how they operate, and the advantages and dangers they pose to the bitcoin ecosystem.

THE OPERATION OF DECENTRALIZED EXCHANGES

There are various DEX designs, and they all have advantages and disadvantages in terms of feature sets, scalability, and decentralization. Order book DEXs and automated market makers (AMMs) are the two most popular varieties (AMMs). Another popular type is DEX aggregators, which search across various DEXs on-chain to get the best pricing or lowest gas cost for the user's intended transaction.

The high level of determinism attained by employing immutable smart contracts and blockchain technology is one of the key advantages of DEXs. DEXs carry out deals utilizing smart contracts and on-chain transactions as opposed to centralized exchanges (CEXs), like Coinbase or Binance, which use their own matching engine to enable trading. DEXs also give customers the option to trade while maintaining full custody of their money in self-hosted wallets.

Network fees and trading fees are the two main types of expenses DEX users are normally expected to pay. While trading fees are collected by the underlying protocol, its liquidity providers, token holders, or a combination of these organizations as stated by the protocol's design, network fees refer to the gas cost of the on-chain transaction.

An end-to-end on-chain infrastructure with permissionless access, zero single points of failure, and decentralized ownership across a community of distributed stakeholders is the goal of many DEXs. This often means that a decentralized autonomous organization (DAO), made up of a community of stakeholders, governs protocol administrative rights by voting on important protocol choices.

It is challenging to maximize decentralization while maintaining the protocol's competitiveness in a crowded DEX market since the DEX's core development team typically has more knowledge about key protocol decisions than a dispersed group of stakeholders. To boost censorship resistance and long-term resilience, many DEXs choose a decentralized governance structure.

ORDER BOOK DEXS

An essential component of electronic exchanges is an order book, which is a live collection of open buy and sell orders in a market. The internal operations of an exchange use order books to match buy and sell orders.

Due to the requirement that every interaction inside the order book be posted on the blockchain, DEXs have historically been less prevalent in DeFi. Either significantly higher throughput than the majority of current blockchains can manage is required for this, or network security and decentralization must be seriously compromised. Early order book DEXs on Ethereum as a result had poor liquidity and unsatisfactory user interfaces. Still, these exchanges provided a convincing demonstration of how a DEX could support trading using smart contracts.

On-chain order book exchanges have grown more practical and now see a lot of trading activity thanks to scalability improvements like layer-2 networks, optimistic rollups, and ZK-rollups, as well as the introduction of higher-throughput and app-specific blockchains. Hybrid order book designs, in which the management and matching of orders take place off-chain while trade settlement takes place on-chain, have also grown in popularity.

The order books DEXs 0x, dYdX, Loopring DEX, and Serum are several that are well-liked.

AUTOMATED MARKET MAKERS (AMMS)

The most popular sort of DEX is one with automated market makers since it allows for quick liquidity, democratized access to liquidity, and—in many cases—permissionless market creation for any token. A money robot in essence, an AMM is always ready to propose a price between two (or more) assets. An AMM uses a liquidity pool instead of an order book where users can trade their tokens, with the price set by an algorithm based on the percentage of tokens in the pool.

AMMs allow rapid access to liquidity in markets that could otherwise have reduced liquidity since they can always quote a price for a user. A willing buyer must wait for their order to be matched with a seller's order in the case of an order book DEX; even if the buyer puts their order to the "top" of the order book near to the market price, the order may never execute.

In the case of an AMM, a smart contract controls the exchange rate. Users can instantly access liquidity, and liquidity providers—those who deposit funds into the liquidity pool of the AMM—can profit passively from trading commissions. AMMs have seen a huge increase in the number of new token launches thanks to the combination of instant liquidity and democratized access to liquidity provision. This has also allowed for the development of new designs that concentrate on specific use cases, such as stablecoin swaps.

AMMs could be used to support swaps of NFTs, tokenized real-world assets, carbon credits, and much more, even though the majority of existing AMM designs focus on cryptocurrencies. Bancor, Balancer, Curve, PancakeSwap, SushiSwap, Trader Joe, and Uniswap are a few examples of well-known AMM DEXs.

EVOLUTION OF DECENTRALIZED EXCHANGES

Although the first decentralized exchanges originally surfaced in 2014, these platforms didn't really take off until decentralized financial services based on blockchain gained popularity and AMM technology enabled DEXs overcome their previous liquidity issues.

These platforms struggle to enforce Know Your Customer and Anti-Money Laundering checks because no single organization verifies the kinds of data that are typically provided to centralized platforms. However, regulators might try to establish these controls on decentralized systems.

Since these platforms still require users to sign blockchain messages to move money off of them, even those that do allow user deposits are exempt from the regulations that apply to custodians.

These days, decentralized exchanges allow users to lend money to earn interest passively, borrow money to leverage their holdings, or supply liquidity to earn trading commissions. These systems' reliance on self-executing smart contracts may lead to the development of further use cases in the future. Flash loans are an example of how innovation in the decentralized finance sector can produce goods and services that were previously impossible. Flash loans are defined as loans taken and repaid in a single transaction.

WHAT ARE THE BENEFITS OF DECENTRALIZED EXCHANGES?

DEX trades contain strong guarantees that they will execute exactly as the user intended, free from the interference of centralized parties, because they are made possible by deterministic smart contracts. DEXs offer robust execution assurances and enhanced transparency into the underpinnings of trading, in contrast to the opaque execution techniques and possibility for censorship inherent in traditional financial markets.

Due to the absence of custodians and the use of self-hosted wallets by consumers, DEXs reduce counterparty risk. By lowering the amount of cash concentrated in the wallets of a limited number of centralized exchanges, DEXs can help lessen some of the systemic risks associated with the blockchain industry. Prior to its abrupt closure and the loss of hundreds of thousands of bitcoins, the Mt. Gox controlled exchange managed a sizeable part of all Bitcoin trade volume in 2014.

DEXs contribute to wider financial inclusion. Accessing a DEX's smart contracts just needs an Internet connection and a compatible self-hosted wallet, unlike some user interfaces that have restricted access based on a user's location or other criteria. In contrast to a centralized exchange, the onboarding procedure for a DEX is simple and nearly immediate because users can sign in easily using their wallet address.

Trading on decentralized exchanges can be costly, particularly when deals are made at a time when network transaction costs are high. Nevertheless, leveraging DEX platforms has a lot of benefits.

Availability of Tokens

Before listing tokens, centralized exchanges must independently inspect them to make sure they adhere to local laws. New projects will probably list on decentralized exchanges before being made available on their centralized equivalents because these exchanges can support any token created on the blockchain around which they are constructed.

While this may imply that traders can participate in initiatives as early as feasible, it also suggests that many scams are published on DEXs. A common exit scam is referred to as a "rug pull." Rug pulls happen when a project's team dumps the tokens that are meant to provide liquidity in the pools of these exchanges when their price increases, making it impossible for other traders to sell.

Anonymity

On DEXs, consumers' identity is protected when they trade one cryptocurrency for another. Users are not required to go through the Know Your Customer (KYC) standard identification process, in contrast to centralized exchanges (KYC). KYC procedures entail gathering traders' personal data, such as their full legal name and a picture of an identification card provided by the government. DEXs thus draw a sizable population of non-identifiable individuals.

Lowered Dangers to Security

Using DEXs reduces the risk of hacking for seasoned cryptocurrency users who control their assets because these exchanges don't have access to their money. Instead, traders keep their money secure and only use the exchange when they want to. Only the liquidity providers may be at danger if the platform is compromised.

Reduction of Counterparty Risk

When the other party to a transaction defaults on its

contractual duties, it creates a situation known as counterparty risk. This risk is minimized by the fact that decentralized exchanges are built on smart contracts and operate without middlemen.

Users can immediately conduct a web search to determine whether the exchange's smart contracts have been reviewed and can base their decisions on the experience of other traders to make sure there are no additional dangers while utilizing a DEX.

DEX RISKS AND FACTORS TO CONSIDER

Through better execution guarantees, more transparency, and permissionless access, DEXs have democratized access to trade and liquidity provision. DEXs do, however, come with a number of dangers, including but not limited to:

Smart Contract Risk

Blockchains are thought to be quite secure for carrying out financial transactions, however there is a smart contract risk. The level of expertise and experience of the team that created a smart contract does, however, have an impact on the code quality of the project. DEX users may experience a financial loss as a result of smart contract faults, hacks, vulnerabilities, and exploits. By using peer-reviewed code, good testing procedures, and security audits, developers can reduce this danger, but they must always exercise caution.

Liquidity Risk

Even while DEXs are growing more and more popular, certain DEX marketplaces have inadequate liquidity, which causes significant slippage and a bad user experience. Significant sections of trading activity are still undertaken on centralized exchanges, which frequently results in reduced liquidity on DEX trading pairs because of the network effects of liquidity, which work as follows: high liquidity draws more liquidity, low liquidity attracts less liquidity.

Frontrunning Risk

Because blockchain transactions are public, arbitrageurs or bots seeking to extract the most extractable value (MEV) from unknowing users may attempt to frontrun DEX deals. These bots attempt to take advantage of market inefficiencies by paying higher transaction fees and minimizing network delay, much like high-frequency traders do in traditional markets.

Risk of Centralization

Points of centralization can still exist even if many DEXs strive to maximize their decentralization and censorship resistance. These include, among other things, the use of subpar token bridging infrastructure, the hosting of the DEX's matching engine on centralized servers, and administrative access granted to the DEX's smart contracts by the development team.

Network Risk

Using a DEX may be excessively expensive or completely impossible if the network experiences congestion or downtime because the exchange of assets is made possible by a blockchain, making DEX users vulnerable to market fluctuations.

Token Risk

Because anyone can develop a market for any token on multiple DEXs, there is a higher chance of purchasing subpar or malicious tokens than there would be on centralized exchanges. Users of DEX should think about the dangers of taking part in projects in their early stages.

In addition to the aforementioned, some users could find the idea of having complete control over their private keys to be unsettling. One of the key advantages of the Web3 vision is having complete control over one's assets, yet many users might prefer to entrust a third party with that responsibility. While accessing a sophisticated ecosystem of open-source financial services, more users may be able to take advantage of the advantages of preserving total control over their assets by adhering to proper security and key management procedures.

SIX
DECENTRALIZED FINANCE

> *The reason we are all here is that the current financial system is outdated.*
>
> CHARLIE SHREM

A wave of global financial disruption has been sparked by the explosive growth of cryptocurrencies into a trillion dollar sector. Ingenuity dating back to the 1980s and significant developments in cryptography are at the core of the cryptocurrency industry. Since then, a variety of things have changed the crypto world. The first cryptocurrency to arrive, Bitcoin, did so in 2009, and this is the one that stands out the most. Despite Bitcoin's phenomenal rise, financial services have only just begun to be offered, largely because of the cryptocurrency's intrinsic instability and lack of adoption. Due to Bitcoin's high price fluctuation, mainstream institutions won't accept loans made with it. Bitcoin is a bad asset for precisely planning any investment because of this.

In the rapidly evolving world of cryptocurrencies, decentralized finance (DeFi) is a popular movement. Let's explore DeFi further and learn more about it since it is being used in a variety of novel and intriguing ways.

OVERVIEW OF DECENTRALIZED FINANCE (DEFI)

DeFi, which stands for "decentralized finance," is a catch-all word for apps and projects in the public blockchain environment aimed at upending the established financial sector. DeFi refers to financial apps created using smart contracts and blockchain technology. Smart contracts are automated, enforceable contracts that can be executed without the assistance of a third party. They are accessible to anyone with an internet connection and can be used for a variety of tasks, including financial transactions.

DeFi comprises of peer-to-peer protocols and applications built on decentralized blockchain networks with no access rights. Financial instruments can be easily lent, borrowed, or traded using decentralized apps (dApps). The Ethereum network is now used to build the majority of DeFi apps, but a number of new open networks are gaining popularity because of their greater speed, scalability, security, and affordability.

WHAT ARE SMART CONTRACTS?

The majority of smart contracts provide Turing Complete programming languages, enabling numerous parties to communicate with one another decentralized. Blockchains are the best platforms to use for creating financial applications since they can benefit from smart contracts.

HOW WAS DEFI ESTABLISHED?

Central governments have always created the money that supports our economy. The strength of monetary systems increased as people's trust in those currencies expanded. However, because confidence has been betrayed so often, people are skeptical of the centralized authority' capacity to handle the money. DeFi was developed to build an open financial system that reduces the need for reliance on a centralized authority.

DeFi is said to have begun in 2009 with the introduction of Bitcoin, the first peer-to-peer (p2p) digital currency constructed on top of the blockchain network. Bitcoin made it feasible to imagine a change in the status quo of finance. The crucial next step in decentralizing antiquated financial systems is blockchain technology. All of this was made possible by the 2015 release of Ethereum and, more especially, smart contracts. A second-generation blockchain known as the Ethereum network enhances this technology's potential in the financial sector. It encouraged companies and enterprises to develop and implement the projects that made up the DeFi ecosystem.

DeFi provided numerous chances to develop a reliable, open, and uncontrollable financial system. Projects turned a corner in 2017 and started to expand beyond simple money transfers.

THE DIFFICULTIES OF CENTRALIZED FINANCE

Financial markets have the power to foster innovative thinking and promote societal prosperity. Nevertheless, these marketplaces are centralized in authority. People give up their assets to intermediaries, such banks and financial institutions, when they invest in the current financial system. Because of this, the focus of these systems remains on risk and control.

In the past, we have observed bankers and institutions mismanage market risks. A tragic example of this was the financial crisis of 2008. There is little question that when central authorities handle money, risk builds up in the center and puts the entire system in jeopardy.

Initially designed to allow people total control over their assets, early cryptocurrencies like bitcoin were centralized mainly for issuing and storing new coins. Access to a wider range of financial instruments remained difficult until the advent of smart contracts, which allowed for DeFi.

HOW RISKY IS INVESTMENT IN DEFI?

Due to the market's extraordinary volatility and unpredictability, any investment in cryptocurrencies carries a certain amount of risk. Although high earnings on staking or crypto lending may initially sound alluring, the values of the majority of the main cryptocurrencies have fallen noticeably so far in 2022.

As a result of investors selling risky assets like cryptocurrencies due to rising interest rates, the prices of Bitcoin and Ethereum have both fallen by more than 50% year to date. This year, more crypto lenders, stakers, and liquidity miners have lost money on their principal than they have made this year in interest payments.

A liquidity constraint issue also shook the crypto lending industry in 2022. Voyager Digital, BlockFi, and Celsius, three crypto lending services, were even compelled to freeze client assets. BlockFi is having problems as a result of a significant client failing to satisfy a margin call on an overcollateralized loan, while Voyager Digital and Celsius have both just declared bankruptcy.

Unfortunately, there is currently very little regulation in the DeFi space. The Federal Deposit Insurance Corporation, or FDIC, normally provides insurance to investors who receive interest from bank accounts. There is no such safeguard available to DeFi investors.

For many people, DeFi lending is the perfect answer, but there are risks involved. Users of several lending protocols are forced to deposit their money into a liquidity pool, where they are vulnerable to temporary losses. Flash loans, a sort of loan in which money is borrowed and paid back in one transaction, have drawbacks as well. They enable DeFi users to take out substantial cryptocurrency loans that could be used to rig token values.

DeFi technology is still in its infancy and hasn't been completely stress-tested at scale for a long time. Money could disappear or be at risk. Compound, a DeFi platform, recently experienced a significant bug in which clients unintentionally received millions of dollars' worth of cryptocurrency.

Despite inadequate consumer protection and the lack of laws and regulations, DeFi has prospered. But this implies that when anything goes wrong, users frequently have little to no protection. There are no rules requiring capital reserves for DeFi service providers, and there are no state-run reimbursement programs that include DeFi.

Threats come from hackers. Although there is a risk of hacking in traditional finance as well, DeFi's extensive technological architecture, with its numerous possible points of failure, enhances the so-called attack surface that knowledgeable hackers can use. For instance, "white hat" hackers stole $610 million from the DeFi platform PolyNetwork in August 2021 by taking advantage of a smart contract vulnerability. Fortunately, every penny was repaid.

There are strict collateral restrictions. Almost all DeFi lending transactions call for collateral that is at least equal to the loan's value, if not greater. The eligibility for various types of DeFi loans is severely constrained by these conditions.

PREREQUISITES FOR PRIVATE KEYS

Users with DeFi and cryptocurrencies must protect the wallets they utilize to keep their bitcoin assets safe. This is a crucial prerequisite for multi-signature wallet users who are both private investors with their own money and institutional investors. To do this, private keys—lengthy, distinctive codes known only to the wallet's owners—are employed. For instance, if a private investor misplaces their key, they are permanently unable to access their money.

USING DEFI

Anyone with Internet access can utilize DeFi apps, create and offer services (like loans), and combine existing services because the code is open. DeFi systems and software are freely accessible to the general public and may even be duplicated, improved, or customized to meet specific user requirements.

You will require a virtual wallet to store tokens, the "hard currency" in blockchain that can be purchased with euros, dollars, and other forms of legal tender, in order to access DeFi apps. Users of the DeFi app can create a smart contract to sell bitcoin at a specified price in order to earn a return on their token investments. Users can create a smart contract to automatically acquire tokens when they reach the desired value if they want to purchase them. There is no middleman, and transactions are automatic in both scenarios.

It is unregulated since it is a decentralized financial environment. According to the conventional financial system, personal information can be examined to evaluate loan applicants' debt and other factors. The "identifier" on blockchain, however, is a public key that does not contain any personal data. This can make it difficult to avoid fraud and other financial crimes.

Security is another crucial element. Users protect their own assets on DeFi platforms by using access keys and authentication to log in to apps. Users risk losing all of their assets if their personal information is taken because no one can provide or restate it.

Smart contracts are pieces of code that are kept on blockchain networks and that automatically execute contracts when specific criteria are satisfied. These contracts instantaneously carry out an agreement with a predetermined result without the need for a middleman, like a bank, broker, or lawyer.

Many conventional economic transactions, according to proponents of the DeFi system, can be self-executed through the use of smart contracts in a quicker, less expensive, simpler, and more secure way.

The DeFi system is made up of a number of loan platforms, exchanges, and individual players that operate independently, decentralized from the traditional financial system, and without a centralized authority. The DeFi industry is frequently referred to as the "Wild West" of finance because it is still somewhat unregulated and young.

HOW CAN INVESTORS PROFIT FROM DEFI?

Investors can profit from the DeFi market in a variety of ways. First, just like stock traders trade shares of Apple Inc. (ticker: AAPL) and Microsoft Corp. (MSFT) in their brokerage accounts, investors may trade cryptos, non-fungible tokens, and other digital assets on decentralized exchanges. Users of DeFi can also make money by lending, staking, or mining liquidity.

By locking up coins and devoting them to a cryptocurrency system, staking is a method for investors to earn interest on some cryptocurrencies. These staked currencies serve as the basis for transaction validation in cryptos like Cardano (ADA), Solana (SOL), and Polkadot (DOT) that employ a proof-of-stake consensus process. When chosen to validate a block of transactions, entities that stake coins can become transaction validators, and validators are rewarded with cryptocurrency.

Users stake their cryptocurrencies to earn interest. This interest is comparable to the interest that they would receive from a conventional savings account, but the rates obtained through staking are frequently substantially greater than the savings rates currently provided by banks.

The process of adding cryptocurrency assets to a liquidity pool in order to support trades and transactions inside a DeFi protocol is known as "liquidity mining." Liquidity mining players essentially earn interest on their donations because they share in the platform's fees or new tokens in return for their contributions to a liquidity pool.

Finally, investors have two options: they can directly lend out cryptocurrency or store it in an interest-bearing account on a platform for crypto lending, like an exchange or the DeFi app. While some cryptocurrency lending accounts provide variable interest rates, others offer fixed rates based on a predetermined lockup time.

DEFI PROTOCOLS AND THEIR OPERATION

DeFi has developed into a full ecosystem of functional protocols and applications that benefit millions of users. By April 2022, DeFi ecosystems had approximately $239 billion in assets locked up, making it one of the public blockchain space's fastest-growing categories.

The Most Common DeFi Use Cases and Protocols
Blockchain Oracle

Real-world data must be connected to the blockchain for some decentralized applications. Prediction markets, for instance, consider real-world events like elections as financial goods and demand that the real-world data be held on-chain in order to distribute payments to those who correctly forecasted the results.

The blockchain is linked to the outside world by an oracle. They are frequently used to transport data from the real world to the blockchain, but they can also send data the other way around. The majority of the time, open APIs are connected by software oracles. Sometimes, physical sensors are employed in hardware oracles to measure things like wind speed.

Consensus oracles are frequently used in protocols to filter out "bad data." To arrive at a single data point, these oracles combine information from many sources and apply a consensus procedure.

DeFi Borrowing and Lending

Users can earn annual yields by lending others their cryptocurrencies through decentralized lending. Decentralized borrowing enables anyone to take out loans at a set interest rate. These DeFi protocols enable peer-to-peer lending, which does not require middlemen like traditional finance does.

Users don't have to wait to receive their funds because DeFi lending protocols use an automated smart contract code to enable loans. Additionally, these protocols do away with the requirement for credit checks and let anyone, anywhere, borrow cryptocurrency. In order to protect themselves against volatility, some decentralized lending systems provide rate-switching capabilities that allow borrowers to switch between variable and stable interest rates.

WHAT CHALLENGES DO DEFI PROJECTS FACE?

A lot of the issues and dangers a DeFi project faces are connected to the technology that underpins them—blockchains. Since the Ethereum blockchain serves as the foundation for more than 90% of DeFi initiatives, we will refer to the Ethereum problems as DeFi challenges:

1. Uncertainty

A DeFi project will spontaneously inherit any instability present on the host blockchain if that blockchain is unstable. The Ethereum blockchain is still going through a lot of changes. For instance, errors made when switching from the

PoW system to the new Eth 2.0 PoS system could present new risks to DeFi projects.

2. Scalability

The host blockchain's scalability is another significant issue with DeFi systems. The scaling issue leads to two significant issues:

A) Transactions take a while to finalize

B) During periods of congestion transactions are very expensive

While centralized competitors may handle tens of thousands of transactions per second, Ethereum can only handle roughly 13 at full capacity.

3. Issues with Smart Contracts

For many DeFi initiatives, smart contract vulnerability is a significant source of problems. A smart contract's code can lose money if there is even the smallest error.

4. Low Liquidity

One of the most crucial elements for DeFi token-based projects and blockchain systems is liquidity. By October 2020, DeFi will have a total value of over $12.5 billion locked in. When compared to the conventional banking systems, this is a drop in the ocean.

5. Excessive collateralization

The cryptocurrency lending industry is a lucrative service in DeFi, as we previously stated. However, this company suffers from over-collateralization, which happens when the borrower's staked asset's value is prohibitively large in relation to the loan amount itself. High collateralization is used in DeFi projects to combat the removal of barriers like low credit ratings.

6. Limited Cooperation

There are various blockchain architectures, each with its own DeFi environment and community, including Bitcoin, Ethereum, and Binance Smart Chain. DeFi platforms, tools, DApps, and smart contracts on several blockchains may communicate with one another because of interoperability. Many projects are compartmentalized until this is made easy.

7. Inadequate Insurance

Investors are safeguarded by insurance in the case of hacking or other fraudulent activity. In contrast to DeFi, where insurance is significantly more uncommon, centralized finance places a high value on it.

8. Concentration

The primary goal of bitcoin and blockchain was to create a decentralized financial system, however sometimes that system isn't as decentralized as it should be. The likelihood of fraud is significantly reduced by decentralization.

It was a DeFi initiative, "SushiSwap." On September 5, 2020, the SushiSwap project's unknown founder will change all of his Sushi tokens to ETH. After the SUSHI token branched from the Uniswap protocol, its value increased to $10, but it later decreased to $0.6 (at the time this book was being written). This served as an illustration of how a single point of failure is still conceivable in DeFi.

9. The Duty of Investors

Even if DeFi were risk- and problem-free, it wouldn't be accountable for your errors. DeFi shifts accountability from middlemen to end users. In the DeFi space, developing some solutions to prevent human errors and blunders is crucial because if you lose your money accidentally, no one will be liable. Many users are not accustomed to having to take care of themselves in this way, which can result in them losing money or falling victim to scams. Freedom comes with a lot of responsibility.

DeFi is a new and experimental technology with some flaws, particularly in terms of security. Decentralized finance proponents and supporters believe that these issues will eventually be resolved.

THE IMPORTANCE OF DEFI

DeFi provides a wide range of useful use cases, many of which are inaccessible to traditional fiat-based financial systems. Here are a few advantages of DeFi:

DeFi is inclusive and without restrictions. Anybody, everywhere, with a crypto wallet and an internet connection can use DeFi services. Additionally, users don't need to wait for bank transfers or pay traditional bank fees to conduct transactions or move their assets. (However, other crypto-specific fees, like gas fees, might be necessary.)

Real-time transactions take place. Interest rates are changed numerous times each minute, and the underlying blockchain is updated each time a transaction is completed.

Transparency exists in transactions. More than 90% of all DeFi traffic is sent through the Ethereum blockchain, where every transaction is broadcast to and validated by other users. Any user can view network activities thanks to this level of transaction data transparency.

Using non-custodial cryptocurrency wallets or smart contract-based escrow, users can maintain custody of their assets.

Smart contracts can be created to automatically execute

based on an endless number of variables and are extremely customizable.

DeFi data is safe, auditable, and impervious to tampering thanks to the usage of blockchain technology.

DeFi protocols are frequently open source. The code used to create Ethereum and other projects is open-source, making it possible for anybody to access, check, and modify it. Without requesting permission, developers can quickly integrate various DeFi applications built on open-source technology to produce new financial services and products.

No More Human Errors and Poor Management

We have already mentioned that central banks' (CBs') and third-party intermediaries' (TPIs') incompetence led to financial crises. But because of smart contracts, daily human error is eliminated from the process—unless the contracts were improperly drafted.

Permanent and Quick Access

Before DeFi, you would have to visit a bank and waste a lot of time if you needed a loan. Even late at night, you can apply for a loan with DeFi with only one click. As long as you have an internet connection, you can access the market at any time and from any location.

SEVEN
BLOCKCHAIN/CRYPTOCURRENCY WALLETS

> *Blockchain technology isn't just a more efficient way to settle securities. It will fundamentally change market structures, and maybe even the architecture of the Internet itself.*
>
> ABIGAIL JOHNSON

Users can store and manage their Bitcoin, Ether, and other cryptocurrencies using a blockchain wallet, which is a digital wallet. As a software firm formed by Peter Smith and Nicolas Cary, Blockchain offers a wallet service under the name Blockchain. A blockchain wallet enables cryptocurrency transfers and offers the option to convert received funds back into the user's home currency.

A blockchain wallet enables you to maintain and use your cryptocurrencies and other blockchain-based digital assets, just like a conventional wallet does for your cash. People who possess cryptocurrencies should be knowledgeable about blockchain wallets and how they work because cryptocurrencies are increasingly being used as a form of financial asset, a method for making digital payments, and a tool for the digital economy. Users can send, receive, store, and exchange value on a blockchain using a blockchain wallet. Users can also keep track of and manage the value of their assets on the blockchain.

This chapter goes into great length on what a blockchain wallet is, how it functions, and how to utilize one. We'll witness wallet advancements under the section titled "types of blockchain wallets" as technology develops and new innovations are created. The advantages of using a blockchain wallet will finally be covered, along with some advice on how to make the most of them and stay out of trouble.

FEATURES OF BLOCKCHAIN WALLETS

A blockchain wallet is computer software that operates on a blockchain and holds both private and public keys, as well as keeping track of and recording all transactions involving those keys. A blockchain wallet should ideally not hold any cryptocurrency; instead, all of the information regarding these keys should be kept on the blockchain that the wallet is housed on.

What it really implies is that the wallet offers an ID to make it possible to track all transactions linked to that ID. The blockchain wallet address, which is linked to both the public key and the private key, is the blockchain ID.

Users can store, send, receive, and manage their digital assets on the blockchain using blockchain wallets. One or more forms of blockchain assets, such as Bitcoin, Ethereum, Litecoin, etc., can be stored, sent, received, and managed using this tool.

The following are the fundamentals of blockchain wallets:

The wallet should have all the capabilities required for managing and keeping the assets securely, as well as connecting with other wallets on the same or different blockchains.

For security purposes, a wallet's transactions are all cryptographically assigned.

Blockchain wallets can be used as browser plugins and extensions, as well as on PCs, smartphones, and other devices.

Wallets are private, despite the fact that anyone can download and install the program on their devices. After installing, the user must set up a personal wallet with a password, a distinctive identity, and other security features. Only after gaining access to the wallet to demonstrate ownership may the user conduct transactions from or with it. However, just like sending money to someone using their bank account, you can transfer them cryptocurrency or other digital assets using their wallet ID solely.

Modern cryptocurrency wallets include built-in APIs for obtaining data from other systems. Others can pull data to enable charting and cryptocurrency market analysis, social features to allow emailing and chatting with other users online or posting status updates as well as following and copying their trading practices, and transaction tracking including reading history, prices for different cryptocurrencies. These features help users make profitable trading decisions for cryptocurrencies.

BLOCKCHAIN WALLET ADDRESS

A wallet address looks like this: 16KRo4Zfp7f5tGwdoKCAn-LJXj1PVSbOnDl

While a blockchain is used for software, a personal blockchain wallet is identified by a 32-character address that is generated at random, much like how a bank account is identified by its account number. These addresses can be created, and numerous addresses can be created using a blockchain wallet.

Most wallets will automatically generate a new address for each new transaction in order to keep wallet transactions private. Assets sent or received to previously used addresses will, however, still wind up in the same wallet for the user. With the ability to track all transactions in all the addresses you have ever used, wallets preserve a record of every transaction for each address and increase transparency.

THE CREATION OF A BLOCKCHAIN WALLET ADDRESS

With a wallet, creating a public wallet address is simple, but connecting it to the public key requires mathematical calculations. A public key is used to create a wallet address. For instance, each Bitcoin wallet has the ability to create a P2PKH address (P2PKH is an abbreviation for Pay To Public Key Hash).

Although it was possible to send or pay Bitcoins directly to an Internet IP address, this feature was deactivated after it became evident that such payments would frequently be the target of man-in-the-middle attacks.

Now, a Bitcoin wallet can discover as many P2PKH

addresses as it can, ideally by combining a number of ordinary cryptographic procedures. The ECDSA cryptography algorithm is used by bitcoin.

In a blockchain, hashing the public key using cryptographic algorithms and other conversions should provide the wallet address. The wallet address adds a checksum to protect users from making typing mistakes and reflects the public key in a more accessible manner.

Ideally, a public key and a cryptographic technique are used as the first two steps in creating a wallet address. In various blockchains, the hashing yields different outcomes.

For instance, P2PKH addresses include a "1" at the beginning and four checksum bytes at the conclusion because they are hashed using the RIPEMD-160 algorithm. The first four bytes of the output are hashed twice with the SHA256 method to get the four checksum bytes.

When sending cryptocurrency, the checksum helps users avoid typos. For instance, the system should perform the verification when a user who wants to transmit crypto pastes the address into the address entry. It verifies that the prefix and checksum match those of the address supplied into the entry by checking the prefix and computing the checksum. It is impossible to transfer money to the incorrect address when a typo is made since the system rejects the pasted address if they do not match.

P2PKH addresses may be supported by Bitcoin wallets, however, other blockchain wallets employ different address types to enable more flexible payment ways to validate transactions transmitted via a generated private key on these blockchain networks.

Multiple wallet address types can be supported by a

blockchain wallet to increase the wallet's usefulness. One illustration is the addition of P2SH addresses to the P2PKH addresses supported in Bitcoin wallets. Pay to Script Hash is referred to as P2SH. With the help of this functionality, payments can be sent to script hashes rather than public key hashes. The P2SH is an addition, however, the P2PKH addresses are still supported. In the P2SH scenario, the sender must sign each transaction with a script, and the recipient must confirm that the script being sent matches the hash of the script.

P2PKH addresses are supported, which enables the usage of multi-signature addresses and other techniques in blockchains.

A transaction using a multi-signature address must be signed by two or more parties who both possess private keys in order for it to be considered valid. For example, the funds of a group or organization may be protected by the signatures of two individuals or two witnesses. For multi-signature addresses, two parties each submit a portion of the required script. These addresses begin with a "3" because they utilize the prefix 05 in Bitcoin, for example.

A blockchain network can employ a new RIPEMD-160 algorithm prefix to produce wallet addresses that begin with a different character. For instance, alternative coins like Dash, Litecoin, and Dogecoin use a different prefix of the RIPEMD-160 to start with a different character at the start of their addresses instead of using the prefix "1" as their starting character. Once more, different blockchain networks may produce their private and public keys and wallet addresses using various cryptographic techniques.

HOW A BLOCKCHAIN WALLET WORKS

Cryptography, which protects blockchain wallets, starts with the creation of a set of keys known as the public and private keys. These are used to mathematically secure the cipher.

(i) When you share your wallet address with someone, they will always assign any coins or cryptocurrencies they transfer to you to your public address. The public address is a hashed version of your wallet address rather than your actual wallet address. The input is encrypted using a hash function and transformed into an output known only to you and your wallet and linked to a public address.

(ii) Your private key is the only one that can be used to decrypt the data encrypted by the sender of the coins and unlock the contents of the wallet because it is linked to the public key and, consequently, the wallet address. You can access your coins in this way.

(iii) In order to send cryptocurrency, the wallet's owner must sign a transaction using their private key and submit it to the blockchain network. Once the transaction has been made public, the network's nodes, which operate as verifiers, will utilize the related, publicly available public key that was used to sign the transaction to check that it is genuine and legitimate before allowing it to proceed.

Even when the same private key is used to generate numerous signatures, keep in mind that each transaction generated by the private keys contains a distinct digital signature that makes it difficult to copy or be similar to the others. Users are advised to only use each address once in order to protect their anonymity and boost transaction security.

(iv) The fact that the cryptocurrency sent is assigned by the sender to their public key, which is connected to their wallet address, also serves to authenticate the recipient of the transaction. The sum and the sum reflected in the wallet are unlocked using the recipient's private key. It indicates that the user who owns the private key associated with the public address to which the cryptocurrency was assigned is authorized and has the right to spend the cryptocurrency.

(v) To make trading cryptocurrencies easier, cryptocurrency exchanges and other platforms use this concept. When sending messages through a wallet, the user will also sign the message with their private key.

TYPES OF BLOCKCHAIN WALLETS

Hardware wallets and software wallets are the two primary categories of wallets. Online and offline wallets are subdivisions of the two primary wallets.

Online wallets are connected to the Internet and are commonly used. They are less safe than offline wallets. Offline wallets are used to sign transactions and store private keys without a need for an internet connection. Both paper wallets and all hardware wallets are included.

Deterministic and non-deterministic wallets are divided into different categories based on whether there is a relationship between the public and private keys or not.

Nevertheless, wallets can be classified into different categories based on the platforms they can be used and stored on. Based on the technology they employ, we also have a variety of blockchain wallet types.

1. Non-deterministic Wallets

These are the kinds where the private keys produced by the

wallet are unrelated. Although the wallet allows for the generation of several private keys, the lack of relationship between the keys—for example, the lack of a common recovery phrase or seed—can be a management issue. It's important to backup each key, which causes management issues as you add more keys.

2. Deterministic Wallets

These are those whose wallet-generated private keys are all linked to one another via a recovery seed (24-words long recovery phrase). The only thing a user needs to do to retrieve all of the private keys is to backup the wallet with the seed. Nowadays, deterministic wallets are the norm.

To create all the private keys in deterministic wallets, a single hash function is used as the seed. The wallet and all of the addresses and private keys it contains can be recovered using the seed. Sub-wallets in hierarchical deterministic wallets are connected by a child-grandchild relationship. These kinds of wallets support the BIP-32 standard, which enables this kind of connectivity between the wallets and sub-wallets. In an administrative situation, where a business might want to distribute keys to its various divisions and branches to assist manage costs, this form of HD wallet can be useful.

3. Hardware Wallets

These are physical objects that are used to maintain and store private keys, public addresses, and transaction signatures. The majority of hardware wallets are OLED-screen USB-like gadgets that are used to monitor activity. Using the side buttons, you may scroll around the interface, choose features you want to utilize, and sign transactions.

These tiny devices—about the size of a finger—use USB to connect to computers and other portable devices. They include native desktop applications for several cryptocurrencies. With these apps, they sync.

Although they are more expensive—around $70-$150—hardware wallets are the most secure kinds of cryptocurrency wallets. They keep the keys offline, which explains why. Trezor and Ledger are two examples, both of which let you store more than 22 cryptocurrencies, including BTC and more than 500 ERC-20 tokens. The best candidates for hardware wallets are major organizations that own or manage significant amounts of wealth in cryptocurrency.

4. Paper Wallets

Owners of cryptocurrency must safeguard their private keys. Printing the keys on a piece of paper and storing it in a secure location to use later when spending your cryptocurrency is a smart alternative.

These are some of the safest ways to secure cryptocurrencies, however, if a paper is not adequately secured, it can quickly deteriorate or be accessed by a third party. Paper wallet alternatives are not available for all cryptocurrencies. When storing your Bitcoins or other cryptocurrencies for a very long time, using a paper wallet is strongly advised.

Depending on the cryptocurrency in issue, a paper wallet can be made in a variety of ways. Offline creation is a possibility. For instance, all you have to do to make a Bitcoin paper wallet is download and save bitaddress.org, open the website while not connected to the Internet, and then hover the mouse over the screen to get a random number with a probability of 100%. When you select the paper wallet option on this page, a paper wallet containing one or more wallet addresses and their private keys will be generated. Print off this document and store the main part somewhere safe and secure. Once you have their private keys in your possession, you can use these addresses to store Bitcoin with confidence. A password can be used to safeguard a paper wallet with an additional degree of protection.

5. Desktop Wallets

Desktop wallets are a form of program that may be used with Windows, Mac, and Linux, three of the most popular PC-based operating systems. In almost every other cryptocurrency, the first step is to create a desktop-based wallet. Additionally, desktop wallets have plugins and extensions for web browsers. These consist of the Chrome Extension from Jaxx and the MetaMask Ethereum wallet. Because your desktop or laptop will connect to the Internet, and because their security can be hacked online if used without adhering to strict internet security procedures, they are not the most secure solutions. Utilizing current antivirus software, anti-malware software, and robust firewall processes are some of these precautions.

Overall, additional security and protection measures will be needed for software that connects to the internet. Desktop wallets come in Electrum, Bitcoin Core, and Exodus varieties.

6. Mobile Wallets

Mobile wallets are set up on Android, iOS, or other portable devices as phone applications. To some extent, browser extensions and plugin wallets that are compatible with these devices can be categorized as "mobile."

They make it possible to utilize cryptocurrency while on the road, but because the devices are constantly connected to the internet, they are not the most secure wallets. Some devices enable users to save private keys offline. Software for mobile wallets like Coinomi, Electrum, and Mycelium are a few examples.

7. Web Wallets

One type of hot wallet that is constantly linked to the Internet is the web wallet. The user opens the website wallet URL and logs in to the Internet to run these applications on browsers. As a result, Internet Explorer, Firefox, and Google Chrome can all access them.

Some of these wallets do allow users to keep keys offline, however, most of them store private keys online on the servers where these apps are hosted. Examples of non-hosted wallets that let users download and store keys offline include MyEtherWallet and MetaMask. These wallets do not store keys on servers. Examples of hosted wallets are Coinbase and CEX.io.

8. Single or Multi Currency Wallets

In contrast to multi-currency wallets, single currency wallets only hold one cryptocurrency. Anyone working with various crypto types may find using multicurrency wallets to be easier since they eliminate the need to install separate wallets for each. These could be extensions or plugins, hardware, web, or mobile wallets.

CREATION AND USAGE OF A BLOCKCHAIN WALLET FOR CRYPTO TRANSACTION

Blockchain wallet addresses can be created offline using websites like bitcoinaddress.org and BitHalo for multi-signature addresses or online using a wallet. Downloading the cryptocurrency's native wallet application and setting a wallet address are the first steps in building a wallet for the majority of cryptocurrencies. A user must register and create an account for some, but not all. Before you can access your wallet and send cryptocurrency there, hosted wallets on centralized exchanges need you to sign up with an email address and a name, complete KYC procedures, and then verify your information.

Most wallets will let you download and keep your private key as a Keystore file on your device once you download the software and get a wallet address, or you can write it down and store it in your wallet. In the event that your device is lost, these are used to retrieve your wallet. The wallet account creation process can then be started.

Most wallets provide you with the option of adding extra security measures like passwords and TRUE authentication methods. To access the security function of the wallet and add the wallet authenticator account, all you have to do is download the AUTHY, Google, or other authentication apps to your mobile device. Every time you attempt to log in to the wallet, an access code will be sent to you via the app. One-time links that are sent to your email each time you attempt to sign in to the wallet and that you must click in order to sign in are among the additional features. Mobile-based login codes that are called or texted to your smartphone each time you attempt to log in to the wallet are among the additional security elements.

It is simple to send cryptocurrencies into a wallet since all you need to do is log in, receive your wallet address or create one, and then send your coins to that address. Sending from the wallet entails using the balance by transferring all or a portion of it to an external wallet address, which must support the cryptocurrency you wish to send in order to be functional. If the crypto is sent to the incorrect address, you run the risk of losing it.

FUNCTIONS OF A BLOCKCHAIN WALLET

A digital wallet keeps track of the data encryption required to electronically confirm transactions as well as the individual asset's placement on the blockchain. The two most frequent types of cryptocurrency wallets are those made of hardware and software, often known as cold and hot storage wallets. A cold storage wallet is intrinsically safer than the other one because it is not reliant on the internet. While most digital wallet apps are used to store a variety of different currencies, they may also contain the keys to fungible and exchangeable virtual currencies that signify goods, financial instruments, and services.

BENEFITS OF USING A CRYPTOCURRENCY WALLET

It has become abundantly clear over the last few years that those who continue to invest in virtual currencies have a lot of potential and areas for possible rewards. For most people, keeping and investing in cryptocurrency in a crypto wallet is also a respectable option. The finest cryptocurrency wallets give users the ability to transfer, gather, and keep track of their holdings. This kind of wallet can be useful given that digital currencies can be traded online utilizing blockchain technology, which boosts security. Additionally, custom wallets give users more freedom and flexibility when managing cryptocurrencies.

1. Simplicity and Usability

Using a crypto wallet is quite easy and basic. As you may prioritize the features you want, you can manage many cryptocurrencies with ease. You can select the colors that draw attention to the graphs and how important it is to make assertions. With this change, you can additionally choose the user interface (UI) style that users will see. It's essential for figuring out how usable and effective the software is. It increases user satisfaction and engagement on the website and acts as a call to action for more people to sign up. Additionally, it entails focusing on their attention span as a whole and making the necessary adjustments.

2. A Potential Long-Term Choice

For improvements to emerge on technical developments, it requires time and several research periods. Although cryptos are not yet widely usable, they have spread over the world and are expected to grow greatly in the upcoming years as new transmission systems are currently being explored.

Cryptocurrency wallets are becoming more dependable as more significant businesses accept them as a form of payment. Cryptocurrency wallets may eventually provide a more sustainable alternative for both saving and investing, enabling cross-border transactions.

3. Privacy of Accounts and Transactions

The overall security of a person's crypto wallet should not worry anyone. When you make a transaction using a virtual currency, you would want to be sure that your investment is safe and secure. When you use a virtual or cryptocurrency wallet, you can be sure that your information, identity, and access to your money are secure. Typically, a highly secure sign-in process is used, and you must enter an encrypted login information ID. This can help to ensure that no one else can access your accounts unless you expressly give them permission.

4. Portfolio Management

Given that cryptocurrency is a form of asset, you may want to be able to maintain it in the same manner as you would other assets you own. If you utilize one of these wallets, you'll be able to see your assets and goods in real time. To do this, you will need access to a variety of graphs and other analysis tools for tracking the performance of each of your underlying currencies. You could require this knowledge in the future in order to make wiser financial decisions.

5. Availability of Numerous Different Currencies

One of the main benefits of using a well-known cryptocurrency wallet is that you have a wide range of currency options to choose from when it comes to investing and holding your virtual currencies. Those who have the means to do so will be able to successfully diversify their financial holdings, lowering risk and raising overall earning potential.

EIGHT
DETERMINING THE BEST CRYPTO WALLET FOR YOU

> *When decentralized blockchain protocols start displacing the centralized web services that dominate the current Internet, we'll start to see real internet-based sovereignty. The future Internet will be decentralized.*
>
> OLAF CARLSON-WEE

Right now, you'd undoubtedly want to know which cryptocurrency wallet is best for your needs. Before exploring the options at this time, you should understand how a crypto wallet functions. Public and private keys can be stored in the cryptocurrency wallet. A log of all transactions for the relevant cryptocurrency is created on the blockchain when money is sent to a wallet's public key. Private keys can then be used to access your cryptocurrency. As you can see, the usage of private keys in bitcoin wallets offers the fundamental assurance of safety. When looking for the finest cryptocurrency wallets, however, one may consider inquiries such as "Which is the safest crypto wallet?"

TOP FACTORS TO CONSIDER BEFORE CHOOSING THE BEST CRYPTO WALLET

As you can see, selecting a bitcoin wallet is a rather sensitive topic for people. Cryptocurrency management and storage entail a sizable amount of time, effort, and financial investment; as a result, safe resources are required. The quest for information on how to get a cryptocurrency wallet is gaining traction as cryptocurrency's acceptance continues to soar to new heights. However, before selecting any random crypto wallet to use when interacting with cryptocurrency, you should exercise prudence. Here are some important considerations to make when selecting a cryptocurrency wallet.

1. Reputation of the Wallet

An evaluation of the wallet's reputation would be the first and most important response to the question, "How can I get a crypto wallet?" To locate the finest cryptocurrency wallet that meets your needs and tastes, you must put in enough research work. When selecting a crypto wallet for the first time, beginners should stick with the well-known options. By keeping an eye out for a few key characteristics, you may quickly identify the most well-known bitcoin wallets.

Testimonials, global recognition, accreditations, and awards for the organization are some of the important signs that can highlight the reputation of a bitcoin wallet. Only after doing an extensive study on the wallet's creators can you identify the finest cryptocurrency wallet.

Verify the founders' credentials and their accomplishments

in the crypto industry to determine the legitimacy of the wallet. Additionally, you ought to search the wallet's history for any evidence of security breaches. At the same time, it is crucial to look into how the business handled the errors and setbacks.

2. Security of the Wallet

You would store your priceless cryptocurrencies in a cryptocurrency wallet, and you have every right to know if the wallet is secure or not. When looking for the best cryptocurrency wallets, most people ask themselves, "Which is the safest crypto wallet?" The highest level of asset protection should be guaranteed when selecting a cryptocurrency wallet. In actuality, your main concern when selecting a bitcoin wallet should be the security of your funds. Nobody wants to spend time and energy learning "How do I get a crypto wallet" only to lose their hard-earned cash. As a result, you must pick a cryptocurrency wallet that ensures your security from hackers. The most crucial thing is that you need reliable evidence that harmful attacks cannot harm your wallet. How do you identify the most secure cryptocurrency wallet for your needs?

The security of a crypto wallet is rated for you using the Evaluation Assurance Level, or EAL. "Which is the safest cryptocurrency wallet?" can be answered without any ambiguity using the EAL rating on a scale of one to seven. Always try to select a wallet with an EAL grade of at least 5. You can have your cryptocurrency stored securely on the servers with full visibility into its movement if the servers have a reliable EAL rating.

3. Facilities for Backup

"Which cryptocurrency wallet is the best?" can be answered by examining the availability of backup facilities, which is the next important consideration. You should be aware that the information in your cryptocurrency wallet is quite valuable. As a result, it's critical to provide sufficient security for the wallet's data. Additionally, cryptocurrency owners should be aware of the chance that human error will result in the loss of all wallet data.

As a result, you want to pick a bitcoin wallet with a reliable backup system. When you inadvertently lose your wallet data or the device is damaged, the backup mechanism will be useful for recovery. The simplicity of the cryptocurrency wallet backup process should be your first priority. Along with providing a password, a passphrase, and a backup link, make sure the backup functionality is accessible.

The best wallets make managing (backing up) all of your private keys simple. Although having control over your Bitcoin's private keys is essential, doing so can be difficult. There are a few factors making it challenging:

First, for the majority of individuals, writing down private keys on paper and storing that paper in a secure location is the safest way to save them. Second, you might wish to carry multiple wallets. For instance, you might want a wallet for savings and another for spending, and you'll need to manage a different private key for each wallet.

You will have at least one private key for each coin you have in your wallet, if you have more than one. Managing all of your keys might be a lot of effort if you start trading numerous cryptocurrencies. The process is greatly facilitated by a wallet with private key management tools, also referred to as backup features.

4. Compatibility

Compatibility is a powerful feature to search for in the

ideal crypto wallet. Compatibility with various devices is the quality of a good bitcoin wallet that is most obviously present. For instance, you require a wallet that performs equally well on several operating systems, like Windows, Linux, iOS, and Android. The device or operating system you are using should be compatible with the cryptocurrency wallet. Additionally, choosing the best bitcoin wallet involves more than just considering compatibility with the supported systems.

When choosing a crypto wallet, you should also consider interoperability with various coins. Determine the types of cryptocurrencies it supports before attempting to learn how to acquire a cryptocurrency wallet. You should make sure that it offers support for further emerging digital currencies in addition to numerous cryptocurrencies. You are less likely to run into problems accessing cryptocurrency when you locate a cryptocurrency wallet that supports numerous coins and is compatible with multiple systems.

5. User Experience

The user experience is a key consideration in the choice of a crypto wallet. You cannot use a cryptocurrency wallet to its full potential if you are not at ease utilizing and knowing how it works. When this happens, you should research the best bitcoin wallets from the standpoint of user experience. Before selecting a crypto wallet, you should consider what users think about it.

Look for user testimonials about a crypto wallet's usability and check the wallet's characteristics. Verify the display size and the wallet's interface before using. Make sure the cryptocurrency wallet has an intuitive, well-organized user interface. The crypto wallet should facilitate simpler navigation in addition to offering a simpler connection with various cryptocurrencies and financial systems.

6. Access to Private Keys (Owning Your Bitcoin)

Make sure your wallet gives you access to your private keys because, theoretically, you cannot control your bitcoin if you do not have access to its "private keys."

The private keys for Bitcoin addresses are 12- or 24-word passphrases created at random, and each Bitcoin address has a unique private key (passphrase). Anyone with access to an address' private key has full control over the Bitcoin linked to that address. This means that if you use a wallet that prevents you from accessing your private keys, you only have a claim to your bitcoin; it is in the custody (and control) of someone else. Likely, you won't ever see your bitcoin again if, for instance, your custodian files for bankruptcy.

Furthermore, if you don't manage your bitcoin's private keys, you must request authorization from the custodian each time you wish to use it (such as sending it) (since the custodian is the one in control). The custodian might, for instance, delay your transmit request for several days and charge you extra fees only to "allow" you to utilize your bitcoin. In contrast, there is no intermediary when using private keys because you are engaging directly with the public blockchain of Bitcoin.

7. Multisig (Shared Wallets)

The "multisig" option in a wallet is a wonderful feature to have. A multisig wallet is one that needs multiple signatures to authorize transactions. You choose 1) how many participants each multisig wallet has, and 2) how many of those participants are necessary for transaction approval. For instance, a "3 of 6 multisig wallet" would contain six users, and any transaction would need to be approved by at least three of them. A transaction may be proposed by any one of the six participants, but at least three must "sign" or authorize it.

This function can be used to increase wallet security. Consider a multisig wallet wherein two of the three participants must agree before a transaction can be approved. In the event that one of the three people misplaces their private key, this would safeguard your money. Additionally, it would safeguard your money in the (very rare) case if one of the three individuals were abducted by bitcoin criminals.

The administration of an organization's treasury is the other important use case for a multisig wallet. The wallet can be configured in this case so that, for instance, three out of six board members would need to sign a transaction to authorize a spending request.

SAFEGUARDING YOUR CRYPTO WALLET

Technology has improved our environment, but it has also increased our individual responsibility for protecting our online security. Today, we witness an increase in malicious actors aiming to defraud the defenseless using crypto phishing attacks.

The phone-porting attack is one common crime committed against cryptocurrency traders. Criminals search social media for cryptocurrency discussions where participants post their email addresses and phone numbers to facilitate quick connections. After that, hackers call the phone company while pretending to be a victim, use various social engineering techniques, and convince the customer service agent to transfer the phone number to a phone under their control. As soon as hackers gain control of the phone number, they access the victim's exchange account or wallet, reset the password, and then steal all of the money in the account.

The lack of a phone number is not the only security flaw. Your home computer could be compromised by hackers. Ransomware, Ponzi schemes, and phishing scams are all common types of bitcoin fraud and theft. The theft of $5,000 worth of Bitcoin by hackers from his account is the fastest way to teach someone about security. Once this occurs, people frequently take security very seriously.

What is the best way to prevent hackers from accessing your cryptocurrency assets? We must acknowledge that there is no perfect solution to the issue. Hard drives, laptops, and smartphones are quickly replacing bank vaults in this digital age. For virtual money, practical knowledge and an awareness of how to keep money safe from thieves are insufficient.

1. Start with a Secure Foundation for Your Wallet

Never install a wallet on a rooted device, and be sure it's malware-free. You should only download the App from the links on official website to ensure that you are always utilizing a genuine copy of wallets.

2. Never Share Your Private Key or Recovery Phrase With Anyone

Your recovery phrase is just as secure as how well you guard it; never reveal it to anyone. To prevent unauthorized access to your wallet, it is crucial to keep it private and secure.

3. Keep a Copy of Your Recovery Phrase Offline

Always maintain an offline copy of your recovery phrase! The simplest solution is to put it in writing on a sheet of paper. Take a look at CRYPTOTAG 1.7k and their products if you want something more robust than paper. It also functions with a text file that is encrypted and kept on a USB drive. You can create a digital backup of your recovery phrase (as well as any other password you select) with the use of a "Password Manager," which you can then keep on one or more USB drives.

4. Separate and Safeguard Your Assets

Use hardware wallets or cold storage. You can utilize hot wallets like Trust Wallet for smaller amounts and 2.9k to store significant quantities of your cryptocurrency.

5. One Recovery Phrase, One Wallet

Never use the same recovery word across multiple wallets. It's best to just use one recovery word per wallet.

6. No Reset or Recovery Procedure Exists so Always Maintain a Backup

Never forget to store a copy of your recovery phrase on backup media. The recovery phrase can always be used to restore your wallet on another phone in the event that your phone is lost, stolen, broken, or the app is unintentionally deleted. There is no way to restart or recover; if you lose your term, you also lose your money.

7. Enable Passcode or Touch/Face ID

Make sure to add a second layer of authentication, such as a Passcode or Touch/Face ID, in order to access your Trust Wallet mobile app so that only you can do so. In the event that you misplace your phone or just leave it at the table while obtaining a cup of coffee for yourself, this stops criminals from getting access to your wallet.

8. Use Strong and Unique Passwords

In 63 percent of all successful cyberattacks, passwords are used. Your chances of getting hacked greatly increase if you use guessable passwords or, worse yet, re-use the same password. It simply isn't worth it to be lazy or use shortcuts when it comes to passwords. Use a password organizer like LastPass if you're not confident in your memory for passwords.

For good reason, a lot of cryptocurrency exchanges, like Bitfinex, now require their users to use two-factor authentication. Use two-factor authentication (2FA) to secure your cryptocurrency wallet, exchange account, email, and any other accounts connected to your cryptocurrency use. However, this second type of authentication should not include SMS verification from a mobile. Attackers with the right motivation may deceive naive customer service representatives into moving a phone number to a new device so they can use it to evade 2FA. Use a 2FA hardware key or a tool like Google Authenticator to safeguard your accounts instead.

9. Regularly Update Your Software

Older software has flaws that hackers can use to access your devices. This holds true for all of your software, not just the crypto software. To keep your data secure, including your cryptocurrency, install patches and updates whenever they become available.

10. Use Multisig and 2FA

With crypto, two-factor authentication is essential. If you want a bitcoin wallet that is really safe, enable multisig transactions.

It should be challenging to access your digital wallet, but not so challenging that you lock yourself out. Everybody occasionally forgets their password. Additionally, there is no "forgot my password" link in crypto wallets, so make sure to create a strong password that you won't forget.

11. Protect Your Email and Devices

The best method to secure your digital currency is to secure your gadgets. Take into account both desktop and mobile defense since one weak point can jeopardize the entire system.

Stop hackers from remotely infecting your Android with malware or gaining access to an email account linked to your cryptocurrency wallet. The CryptoShuffler Trojan and other incursions can be found with malware scanners, protecting your information from being stolen. You could believe that transferring your funds to an offline wallet will provide you with adequate security. However, all your efforts can be in vain if your computer was compromised at the time you set up your Bitcoin wallet.

NINE
THE TOP CRYPTOCURRENCY WALLETS

> *Blockchain is the tech. Bitcoin is merely the first mainstream manifestation of its potential.*
>
> MARC KENIGSBERG

Since most popular exchanges enable you to store your cryptocurrency within your account, much like a 401(k) or IRA does within a Fidelity or Vanguard account, not all cryptocurrency investors technically require their own wallet. Contrary to the regular stock market, however, investors in cryptocurrencies do not have access to strong federally mandated protections. The extra security that comes with having your own wallet may be useful when the value of your cryptocurrency increases.

You might take into account a hot or cold wallet, as well as a wallet provided by your preferred exchange, depending on your investing strategy. Here are some of the top cryptocurrency wallets you can use.

1. Coinbase Wallet

A straightforward hot wallet is advised by experts if you are new to the crypto world. These frequently support a wide variety of tokens and coins and are free, simpler to use, and frequently connected to an exchange.

The prominent Coinbase exchange's Coinbase Wallet is perhaps the best option for newbies. It is easy to use, supports a large number of cryptos, and is noncustodial, allowing you to keep custody of your private keys. Currently, the majority of cryptocurrency investors begin using an exchange-hosted wallet like Coinbase Wallet, which is akin to using "an on-ramp and off-ramp into crypto."

The popular cryptocurrency wallet Coinbase allows users to purchase, trade, transfer, and store digital currencies. In the Coinbase Wallet, you can keep track of all your NFTs and crypto coins in one location. More than 35 million users use Coinbase to buy, trade, store, and earn cryptocurrencies in more than 100 different countries. This crypto wallet supports more than 500 crypto assets and can store digital collectibles and NFTs.

You have access to your wallet's private key since Coinbase Wallet is non-custodial. When you sign up, a 12-word recovery phrase is generated. Additionally, it offers AES-256 encryption for digital wallets, two-step verification, biometric logins, and USD balances that are FDIC-insured.

2. Guarda Wallet

The extremely secure and user-friendly Guardia wallet is a cryptocurrency wallet that enables users to purchase, store, exchange, and profit by staking a variety of digital assets. Guarda Wallet has checked the most security boxes out of all software wallet providers, even though it is one of the newest wallet providers on our list of the best crypto software wallets. Guarda Wallet has also passed our reputation background checks with flying colors.

All customers can manage their bitcoin assets easily thanks to the multi-platform software wallet's availability via a web interface, a Chrome browser extension, a desktop program, or a smartphone.

Guarda provides an easy-to-use and safe user experience, making the wallet's in-app purchase fees reasonable in a sector where security is of the utmost importance.

The Lisboa, Portugal-based Guarda Wallet, which was introduced in 2017 by blockchain development firm Guardarian OÜ, has become the leading cryptocurrency software wallet on the market. Guarda Wallet is a non-custodial, multi-platform software wallet that enables users to manage their digital assets while maintaining total control over their private keys using a web interface, a Chrome extension, on desktop, and on mobile (Android and iOS). Users of the multi-asset wallet can safely store and manage more than 400,000 virtual currencies and tokens because it supports more than 50 blockchain networks.

Guardian OÜ has received a virtual currency service license from the Estonian government, allowing Guarda Wallet to offer regulated in-app crypto trading and services relating to prepaid cards. Despite being the newest addition to our ranking of the top software wallets, Guarda Wallet has all the features a cryptocurrency user might possibly require.

3. Electrum

Since more than 10 years ago, holders of Bitcoin have been able to keep their digital currency with the help of Electrum, a safe, open-source wallet designed only for Bitcoin. To make and receive Bitcoin payments over the Lightning Network, users of Electrum can also open Lightning payment channels. When it originally debuted in 2011, Electrum was one of the earliest Bitcoin wallets. One of the greatest Bitcoin-only wallets available today has withstood the test of time: the desktop wallet.

Users may store, transfer, and receive Bitcoin payments securely thanks to the open-source software wallet. Additionally, Electrum enables users to send and receive bitcoin over the Bitcoin Lightning Network using open payment channels. Beginners can find it difficult to utilize Electrum's simple user interface because it was clearly designed with functionality rather than user-friendliness in mind.

A great wallet for seasoned Bitcoin users is Electrum, which offers a variety of advanced features like multi-signature wallets, variable transaction fees, and compatibility with hardware wallets for ultra-secure cold storage.

4. Exodus Wallet

Exodus wallet is a well-known multi-asset cryptocurrency wallet that offers an easy-to-use interface that allows users to manage their cryptocurrency holdings. Exodus Wallet also gives users the option to buy, sell, and stake their digital assets to generate interest.

Exodus, a Nebraska-based company founded in 2015, offers an extremely user-friendly mobile and desktop cryptocurrency wallet. Users of Exodus Wallet may safely store and exchange 180+ digital assets in a single location. Exodus Wallet offers a variety of in-app applications that enable users to earn staking rewards, earn money by lending crypto assets, learn more about the world of non-fungible tokens (NFTs) on Solana, and more in addition to digital asset storage and an integrated exchange.

Exodus Wallet is most notable for its user-friendly, intuitive user interface, which significantly lessens the complexity of managing a portfolio of crypto assets. The well-known wallet also offers active customer service, configurable send fees, and hardware wallet support for higher security. Exodus Wallet is closed-source software, which means users cannot scan the code for flaws, in contrast to many of its competitors.

A great wallet for beginner bitcoin users is Exodus Wallet. It offers a user-friendly interface and an integrated exchange that is available on PC and mobile, taking care of the most urgent requirements of beginners.

5. Ledger Nano X

The second generation hardware wallet from French firm Ledger, which was introduced in 2014, is the Ledger Nano X. One of the earliest hardware wallets on the market and a leader for many years was Ledger's first cryptocurrency product, the Ledger Nano S.

The Nano X looks like a USB drive and pairs with your device over Bluetooth or USB. This indicates that you can use the wallet without a computer by connecting it to your iOS or Android mobile. More than 1,800 cryptocurrencies are supported. As the Bitcoin community requests support for their preferred cryptocurrencies, this list expands yearly.

The Ledger team developed the Ledger Live software, which offers a user interface for all of your holdings even though the device itself is a cold storage hardware wallet. Users now have the option to manage their portfolios and add new wallets for other cryptocurrencies to their devices.

The most widely used hardware wallets in the market are

ledger wallets, which they have always been. As an alternative to Bluetooth, the Ledger also includes a single USB-C to USB-A connector that enables connection to either a desktop computer or a smartphone.

6. Trezor Model T

An expert consensus holds that a cold storage hardware device is unbeatable if security is your top priority. Move your assets to a hardware device if you wish to assume no security risks. A cold storage solution is the safest place to keep your money, and Trezor is one of the best solutions for cold wallets.

The Trezor Model T physical hardware wallet is a good option for security-conscious cryptocurrency investors, according to experts. It's not inexpensive at $280. A huge, full-color touchscreen display and add-ons like Shamir Backup, a security standard created by Trezor and exclusively available for the Model T, are a few of the Model T's unique features, though. You can build 16 recovery phrases using the Shamir backup to utilize as backups. By enabling you to completely recover your wallet via a recovery seed, the security standard also provides security in the event that it is lost or stolen.

Trezor products are equally as secure as Ledger wallets, but in a few subtle ways, thus it likely comes down to a user's preference. Some people might also prefer the Model T since it is physically stronger and more durable, at least on the outside. Additionally, it is simple to use, straightforward, and easy to set up.

7. Mycelium

Using the industry-leading mobile crypto wallet Mycelium, users can safely manage their Bitcoin, Ethereum, and ERC-20 token holdings. A variety of cutting-edge wallet features, including cold storage integration, spending accounts, and single address savings accounts, are offered by the non-custodial wallet.

Mycelium is a well-known mobile cryptocurrency wallet that was introduced in 2012 by Region Research & Development GmbH, based in Austria. Entropy, Mycelium Gear, and Local Trader are just a few of the cryptocurrency solutions that Megion Research & Development created in the early days of Bitcoin. The company is currently concentrating on "the creation of a Mycelium MEDIA social media hardware and software platform."

Mycelium is a mobile-only, open-source wallet that supports Ethereum, Bitcoin, and a number of other ERC-20 tokens. Although the mobile app's user interface is not very user-friendly for beginners, the app offers several advanced wallet features that seasoned cryptocurrency users value, like the option to set specialized HD spending accounts, single address saving accounts, and in-depth transaction data.

For owners of Bitcoin and Ethereum who want to save their funds in a safe, private mobile wallet, the Mycelium wallet is the best option.

8. MetaMask

If you want to buy and hold, a cold wallet may be useful. But if you want to trade your cryptocurrency, a hot wallet is a necessity because it will make transactions a lot simpler and quicker. In light of this, MetaMask has grown to be popular among cryptocurrency traders because it provides access to new Web3 markets. The best hot wallet for Ethereum is MetaMask.

The largest blockchain, Ethereum, on which MetaMask runs and which can communicate with (NFT exchange) Open-

Sea. The most access to the blockchain is provided via MetaMask.

The Ethereum-based blockchain networks, NFTs, and any Ethereum-based coins can all be accessed through MetaMask. It's a well-liked, simple-to-use wallet that can be used with anything Ethereum-built, which makes up a sizable portion of the Web3 universe. These elements work together to give it an advantage over rival wallets.

Additionally, it's simple for "Web2" customers to transition to Web3 thanks to the availability of the mobile app for both iOS and Android smartphones as well as the web extension for the majority of popular browsers. It can be used to exchange or purchase tokens and crypto, store NFTs and other collectibles, and work in tandem with a hardware wallet (like Trezor or Ledger). Consequently, MetaMask can help you learn more about NFTs and the metaverse.

9. Binance

With a wide range of crypto trading options, Binance is a leading cryptocurrency exchange platform. Changping Zhao, a software developer, created Binance in 2017.

Leading cryptocurrency features like Auto-invest, staking, Defi, Futures and Options, and P2P trading are available in this wallet. Their $100 billion average 24-hour trading volume attests to users' confidence in their system. BNB, their own currency, is one of the top 5 cryptos internationally. The Binance Chain is a Blockchain used by this cryptocurrency exchange.

Your coins are secure thanks to Binance's ultra-secure security technology. It makes use of cold storage, device management, address whitelisting, and two-factor authentication (2FA) verification. The majority of coins—95 percent—are kept in cold storage.

10. Crypto.com

One of the quickly expanding cryptocurrency exchange platforms, Crypto.com, offers more than 250 coins. It offers minimal trading costs and lets users sell, hold, buy, and trade a wide variety of cryptocurrencies. It also provides a decentralized exchange, cryptocurrency credit cards, an NFT marketplace, and a standalone crypto wallet in addition to these.

Additionally, you can earn up to 14.5 percent interest on your cryptocurrency if you retain it for a specific amount of time. Gary Or, Kris Marszalek, Bobby Bao, and Rafael Melo established Crypto in Hong Kong in 2016. It presently has 10 million+ users from more than 85 nations.

Peer-reviewed tools are used to analyze both static and dynamic source code at Crypto.com. It makes use of a bug bounty program, cold storage, and two-step verification. Your USD funds are kept at Metropolitan Commercial Bank, a member of the FDIC, and are insured up to $250,000 if you reside in the United States. Since you will be the owner of those monies, neither Crypto.com nor its creditors will be able to seize your fiat money.

11. Zengo

By removing the private key vulnerability, Zengo is the most secure non-custodial wallet in Web3, making it the simplest yet most safe wallet to invest in cryptocurrencies. Create an account in under 60 seconds to claim ownership of your cryptocurrency.

The first Web3 wallet with encrypted biometric security and no private key vulnerability is ZenGo. Although billion-dollar institutions have been using this technology for years,

ZenGo is the first wallet to offer these cutting-edge security capabilities as a cryptocurrency wallet. The improper administration of private keys has resulted in the loss or theft of NFTs worth millions of dollars. A hacker's biggest nightmare, NFT theft, is eliminated by ZenGo's wallet because there is no private key to misplace or lose. ZenGo supports more than 70 assets, including Bitcoin, Ethereum, and Tezos, and provides live customer care in-app around the clock.

Due to ZenGo's sophisticated security, it is incredibly challenging for hackers to access your wallet. You'll have to use 3FA level security when you sign up. You must then click the link in your email to confirm your registration. Your decryption code will be kept on your cloud storage when you have finished those steps. Last but not least, you must configure your encrypted biometrics. Additionally, using MPC-based cryptography, this wallet is incredibly safe. Additionally, "Chill StorageTM," a guaranteed access option, has been put in place to give you access to your money in emergency situations.

12. Minke

The most user-friendly self-custody wallet app for DeFi on the market is commonly regarded as Minke. With Minke, the first fully created gas-free wallet on Polygon, you can purchase cryptocurrencies and stablecoins in only three clicks using Apple Pay or a local bank transfer. Utilizing the built-in DeFi savings pools, you can save.

Minke is a fantastic option for folks who are new to cryptocurrency because it has a ton of features like an introductory app tour, instructive stories, and a simple fiat on-ramp. Crypto natives will find a lot to like, including access to integrated DeFi savings pools without leaving the app. You can earn the entire interest rate while keeping control of your assets thanks to Minke's integration of Aave and mStable.

Since Minke is a fully self-custodial wallet, you alone always have access to your cryptocurrency, even while using the built-in DeFi savings pools. The savings choices have undergone extensive auditing, and Minke only provides durable, tried-and-true Defi with clear yield structures derived from fees, lending, and borrowing.

TEN
GUIDE TO TRADING CRYPTOCURRENCIES

If crypto succeeds, it's not because it empowers better people. It's because it empowers better institutions.

VITALIK BUTERIN

Everyone seems to be obsessed with trading cryptocurrencies. And why not given the considerable returns? But what does the future of cryptocurrencies look like?. Along with the financial industries, it is also causing disruption in other industries including information technology, healthcare, retail, travel and tourism, and many more. Having cryptocurrency sounds nice, but managing it properly is difficult. People are interested in learning how to trade cryptocurrencies because it is popular.

There are numerous considerations and measures that must be taken in order to trade cryptocurrencies. Before spending time and money in this particular industry, experts advise that it is crucial to acquire an in-depth understanding of cryptocurrencies, crypto exchanges, cryptocurrency security, and all relevant terms. In this booming cryptocurrency market, it is essential to have the correct trading methods in mind and to be conscious of the risk that may materialize at any time. Although trading in cryptocurrencies differs from trading on the stock market, some stock market trading techniques can be used to understand cryptocurrency trading. Therefore, when engaging in crypto trading, knowledge of the stock market may be useful.

OVERVIEW OF CRYPTOCURRENCY TRADING

Let's first define trading so that we may go to trading cryptocurrencies. Trading is the idea of buying and selling assets for financial gain. The trading parties' exchanged goods and services might be considered assets. In this case, we're referring to the financial markets where trading in financial products occurs. These include equities, money, cryptocurrencies, and margin goods, among others. Trading is typically thought of as being short-term, yet many people are misled by this idea. Additionally, we will go into greater detail later on regarding the many types of trading, notably day trading, swing trading, and trend trading.

Trading in cryptocurrencies is purchasing and selling digital currency through a platform or exchange. The most well-known platforms for trading cryptocurrencies include Coinbase, Binance, CoinDCX, etc. The goal of bitcoin trading is to produce lucrative results over a predetermined amount of time. We'll go through how trading is different from investing and how it works in more detail.

DIFFERENCE BETWEEN INVESTING AND TRADING

You must distinguish between cryptocurrency trading and cryptocurrency investment as you learn how to buy and sell these digital assets. Which is superior? The ultimate objective is always the same, regardless of the distinctions: generating a profit. The predicted outcome times, however, are considerably different: in trading, they range from the short to medium term, whereas in investing they span from the medium to long term.

Investors in cryptocurrencies purchase and retain their assets for an extended period, ranging from a few months to years. But cryptocurrency traders hold their holdings for a variety of lengths of time, from a few seconds to several weeks.

Trading is based on the idea of making money within a defined time frame, but investing works when you hold the assets for an extended length of time. We must ignore short-term market swings while making any investment and instead focus on long-term trends. The primary objective of bitcoin investment is to acquire additional coins. For instance, if you paid a given amount for four bitcoins, after a few years, the value of your total investment will rise proportionally to the coin price. However, as trading involves short-term volatility, it is crucial to comprehend the daily market while engaging in trading. Earning dollars or any other currency is the main objective. If you want to succeed in cryptocurrency trading, experts advise knowing the market trends and short-term price trends. It is more akin to purchasing low and selling high when the market is trending in your favor. To make the most money in bitcoin trading, you will need to drop coins frequently.

FUNDAMENTAL ANALYSIS (FA)

A technique for determining the value of a financial asset is fundamental analysis. To assess if the value of an item is fair, a fundamental analyst examines both economic and financial aspects. These may include macroeconomic factors like the overall health of the economy, market conditions, or, if applicable, the operations of the business linked to the asset. And macroeconomics' leading and trailing indicators frequently track this.

Analysts seek to identify whether the asset is undervalued or overvalued after completing the fundamental examination. This conclusion can be used by investors to guide their decisions.

For cryptocurrencies, fundamental analysis may also take into account on-chain metrics, a newly emerging area of data science that focuses on open blockchain data. The network hash rate, top holders, number of addresses, transaction analysis, and many more factors are examples of these indicators. On public blockchains, there is a wealth of data that experts may use to build sophisticated technical indicators that gauge various aspects of the network's general health.

Fundamental analysis is frequently employed in the stock market and on the foreign exchange, but it is less appropriate for cryptocurrencies at this time. There just isn't a defined, all-inclusive framework for evaluating market valuations for this asset class because it is so new. Additionally, a lot of the market is influenced by rumors and stories. As a result, the impact of basic factors on the price of a cryptocurrency is often very small. However, as the market evolves, more precise approaches to considering the price of crypto assets might emerge.

How can one tell if a financial asset is founded on solid principles as opposed to marketing hype, overblown technology, or worse, nothing at all? Considerations for the fundamental study of new assets should include the following:

Developers: Before making an investment in a cryptocurrency asset, it is critical to evaluate the reliability and competence of the developers. What is their history? What software projects have they previously launched? How far along are they in creating the token's underlying protocol? Since many projects are open-source, tools for collaborative code repositories like GitHub make it possible to immediately observe this activity.

Community: For projects involving cryptocurrency trading, the community is essential. The majority of the power behind these assets and the technology that underpins them comes from the combination of users, token holders, and enthusiasts. After all, any new technology always has a social component. However, due to the high stakes involved and the frequent presence of amateur retail investors, the environment is frequently poisonous and riven with rivalries. Therefore, a constructive dialogue within the community is encouraged.

Technical specifications: The fundamental technical requirements for a crypto asset, which should not be confused with market technical analysis, include the network's chosen algorithm (how it maintains security, uptime, and consensus), as well as issuance/emission features like block times, the maximum token supply, and the distribution strategy. A trader can ascertain whether such aspects support a potential investment by carefully examining the protocol stack of a cryptocurrency network and the monetary policy enforced by the protocol.

Innovation: While electronic money was initially meant for use with Bitcoin, developers and business owners have not only found additional uses for the blockchain but have also created entirely new protocols to support a wider range of applications.

Liquidity (and whales): A healthy market requires liquidity. Exist trustworthy exchanges that support a specific cryptocurrency asset? What trading pairs are there if any? Is the volume of trade and transactions healthy? Are there significant market participants, and if so, how do their trading habits affect the market?

Branding and marketing: A new, innovative protocol might already be in use, but it might not have immediate access to liquidity. As a result, generating liquidity takes time. These investments are dangerous. You are effectively gambling that a strong market will someday develop around the project if volumes are low and there are few to no trading pairs available.

This is not meant to minimize the branding and marketing that do eventually result from a process. In fact, a complete picture of how specific actors convey value propositions to the general public may be obtained by comparing the marketing initiatives of core developers, businesses, foundations, and community members.

Infrastructure: This characteristic of a cryptocurrency exchange can be viewed as the expression of a project's technological requirements. What is the actual physical embodiment of the protocol under consideration, despite what is said in white papers or presented at conferences?

It is important to identify the stakeholders, including the developers, block validators, retailers, and users. Furthermore, it is essential to comprehend who the network's stewards are, what they do to secure the network (mining, validation), and how power is divided among them.

TECHNICAL ANALYSIS (TA)

Technical analysts use a distinct methodology. The fundamental tenet of technical analysis is that past price behavior may provide clues as to how the market will probably behave going forward.

Technical analysts don't try to determine an asset's intrinsic value. Instead, they analyze past trading activity and make opportunities-based decisions from there. This can involve examining price movement and volume, as well as using technical indicators, chart patterns, and a variety of other charting tools. This analysis's objective is to assess a market's strength or weakness.

Having said that, technical analysis can be used for more than just forecasting the likelihood of future market moves. The framework can also be helpful for managing risks. Technical analysis makes managing trades more defined and measurable because it offers a paradigm for understanding market structure. The first step in controlling risk in this situation is to measure it. For this reason, not all technical analysts are purely traders. Technical analysis might only be used by them as a foundation for risk management.

Technical analysis is a practice that can be employed in any financial market, and it is very popular among cryptocurrency traders. However, is technical analysis effective? Well, as we've already indicated, speculative activity is largely responsible for the cryptocurrency markets' current valuation. Because they can succeed by just taking into account technical criteria, this makes them the perfect playing field for technical analysts.

ON-CHAIN ANALYSIS

Since blockchain technology underlies all cryptocurrencies, a brand-new sort of analysis that depends on data from blockchains has emerged: on-chain analysis. Analysts are able to make precise qualitative and quantitative observations about the strength of a cryptocurrency's blockchain network and its price dynamics in a range of markets by examining supply and demand trends, transaction frequency, transaction costs, and the rate at which investors are buying and selling a cryptocurrency.

Due to the analysts' ability to correlate numerous macro and microeconomic events with the actions of investors, which are immutably recorded on the blockchain, on-chain data also offers important insight into investor psychology.

Analysts search for abnormalities in the buying, selling, and holding patterns of cryptocurrencies in relation to market rallies, sell-offs, regulatory developments, and other network-oriented events. This is done in order to predict anticipated price changes in the future and investor responses to upcoming occasions like network improvements, halvings of the coin supply, and developments in conventional financial markets.

Which is better technical analysis or fundamental analysis? That is completely dependent on your trading approach. In fact, why not employ both? The majority of market analysis techniques perform best when paired with other techniques or indicators. This increases the likelihood of discovering more trustworthy investment possibilities. Combining various trading approaches can also aid in removing biases from your decision-making.

Confluence is a term that has been used to describe this idea. Confluence traders combine several tactics into one that capitalizes on the advantages of each. It is hypothesized that the trading possibilities offered by the combined techniques may be more potent than those offered by a single approach alone.

ELEVEN
UNDERSTANDING THE CRYPTO MARKET

> *There are 3 eras of currency: Commodity based, politically based, and now, math-based.*
>
> CHRIS DIXON

The truth is that "the market" is just people buying and selling things. To the layperson, "the market" might appear to be some complicated system that only a specialist could ever hope to understand. At first glance, trading cryptocurrencies could appear like a mysterious concept. But once you start to get it, the concept gets a lot clearer.

The sum of all open buy and sell orders represents the state of the market at any particular time. In order to read the market, a trader must continuously look for patterns or trends throughout time and decide whether to act on them.

MARKET TREND

The general direction in which the price of an asset is moving is called a market trend. Technical analysts frequently use price action, trend lines, or even important moving averages to pinpoint market patterns.

Both bullish and bearish market patterns are present overall. A "bullish" market, sometimes known as a "bull market," is one in which price activity seems to be rising gradually. Due to the surge in demand, these price increases are sometimes referred to as "pumps." When the price activity seems to be decreasing consistently, the market is said to be "bearish" or in a bear market. Due to the widespread selling that occurs, these price declines are frequently referred to as "dumps."

Depending on the time period you use, bullish and bearish trends can potentially exist within other more significant opposite trends. For instance, a little short-term bearish trend could develop within a larger long-term bullish trend. Price activity often makes higher highs and higher lows during an uptrend. Lower highs and lower lows are signs of a downtrend.

When the price oscillates back and forth or stays within a range, the market is said to be "consolidating." Consolidation phases typically occur when an item is cooling off after a rapid rising or negative trend, and they are easier to notice on larger time frames (daily charts or weekly charts). Consolidation can also occur prior to trend reversals, during periods of low demand, or when trading volumes are low. During this market condition, prices effectively trade inside a range.

It's important to remember that just because a market trend exists doesn't indicate that pricing will constantly go in that direction. Smaller bear tendencies will be confined by a long-term bull market, and vice versa. Simply said, market trends are what they are. It all relies on the time range you are looking at, thus it all depends on your perspective. Market movements on longer time horizons will always be more important than those on shorter time horizons.

A peculiarity of market trends is that they can only be accurately predicted in the future. You may be familiar with the idea of hindsight bias, which describes a person's propensity to believe they correctly predicted an event before it occurred. As you might expect, the process of determining market trends and making trading decisions can be significantly impacted by hindsight bias.

MARKET CYCLE

The expression "the market goes in cycles" may be familiar to you. A pattern or trend that appears repeatedly is known as a "cycle." Higher time frame market cycles are typically more reliable than lower time frame market cycles. Nevertheless, tiny market cycles can eventually be found on an hourly chart, just as they might be when looking at decades' worth of data.

Traders can see patterns throughout years of varying price activity, just as they do within hours, days, and months of time. The market is susceptible to particular behaviors because of its basic structure.

Four major segments of the cycle can be identified: accumulation, markup, distribution, and decline. Traders will regularly adjust their positions as the market transitions between these phases by consolidating, retracing, or correcting as they see fit.

The behavior of the bear and the bull differ greatly from one another despite existing in the same environment. A trader must be aware of their own role as well as the role that is now saturating the market.

Markets are by nature cyclical. Certain asset classes may outperform others during cycles. Due to various market conditions in other parts of the same market cycle, the same asset classes may perform worse than other types of assets.

It's important to remember that it's difficult to predict where we are in a market cycle at any one time. Only when that phase of the cycle has ended can this analysis be performed with great precision. Additionally, market cycles hardly ever have distinct beginnings and ends. It turns out that being in the present is a very skewed perspective in the financial markets.

CHASING THE WHALE

Price changes are primarily influenced by "whales," or people or organizations with a lot of money to trade. In order to provide liquidity for an asset while making money in the process, some whales engage in "market making," establishing bids and asks on both sides of the market. Whales can be found in almost every market, including stocks, commodities, and cryptocurrency.

The instruments of the trade favored by whales, such as their preferred TA indicators, must be taken into account by a bitcoin trading strategy. Simply put, whales typically have a good sense of direction. A trader can collaborate with these skilled movers to succeed with their own approach by anticipating the intentions of whales.

PSYCHOLOGICAL CYCLES

It can be easy to overlook the fact that, for the most part, real people are behind these trades and that, as a result, they are susceptible to emotional behaviors that can have a major impact on the market when surrounded by a zoo full of metaphors. The well-known chart "Psychology of a Market Cycle" shows this market feature:

Despite the value of the bull/bear framework, the psychological cycle mentioned above offers a more thorough spectrum of market mood. The force of group mentality often takes hold, despite the fact that one of the fundamental trading rules is to leave emotion at the door. Fear of missing out (FOMO) is what is causing those who haven't yet positioned themselves in the market to climb from hope to exhilaration.

Timing an exit before the bears take control and people panic sell requires navigating the valley between euphoria and complacency. Here, it is crucial to take into account high-volume price activity, which can reveal the market's overall trend. Given that the optimum moment to accumulate within a market cycle is during the depression that follows a sharp decline in price, the "buy low" mentality is pretty obvious. The profit increases as the risk does.

In the midst of the barrage of hot opinions and commentary from the media, chat rooms, or purported thought leaders, the challenge for the professional trader is to avoid letting emotion dictate their trading technique. Whales and other individuals who have the power to change the market's pulse frequently manipulate these marketplaces. Do your research and trade cryptocurrencies with conviction.

BASIC TOOLS

To be clear from a macro perspective, one must be able to recognize market cycles and patterns. It is crucial to understand your place with respect to the whole. Instead of paddling aimlessly in the water and hoping for the best, you want to be the seasoned surfer who can spot when the ideal wave is about to come.

But in order to decide on your actual plan, the micro perspective is also essential. Although there are many TA indications, we will only discuss the most fundamental.

SUPPORT AND RESISTANCE

The terms "support" and "resistance," which refer to price barriers that frequently arise in the market to prevent the price movement from moving too far in one direction, may refer to two of the most frequently utilized TA indicators.

The price at which the downward trend frequently pauses because of a surge in demand is the support level. Traders frequently purchase cheap when prices drop, forming a support line. The price level where the rising trend tends to stall owing to a sell-off is known as resistance, on the other hand.

Many cryptocurrency traders place bets on the price's direction using support and resistance levels, changing their strategies as the price level crosses through either of its upper or lower bounds. Traders can enter or exit positions once they have determined the floor and ceiling, which creates a zone of activity. The standard operating procedure is to buy on the floor and sell at the ceiling.

If the price crosses these thresholds, either way, it indicates how the market is feeling generally. New levels of support and resistance frequently appear as the trend breaks through, thus this is a continuous process.

TRENDLINES

Although traders frequently employ the static support and resistance levels depicted above, price movement typically trends higher or lower with barriers altering over time. A series of support and resistance levels may point to a stronger market trend that is depicted by a trendline.

Resistance levels start to form, price movement slows, and the price is pulled back to the trendline while the market is heading upward. As they show a region that helps prevent the price from dropping significantly lower, the support levels of an ascending trendline are of particular interest to cryptocurrency traders. Similar to this, traders will monitor the series of dropping peaks in a market that is heading downward in order to join them together into a trendline.

The history of the market is the essential component. Any support or resistance levels and the trendlines that come from them gain power over time as they recur. As a result, traders will keep track of these obstacles to guide their continued trading approach.

ROUND NUMBER

The obsession with round-number price levels by novice or institutional investors has an impact on support/resistance levels. It can be challenging for the price to rise above this point when a lot of trades cluster around a nice round number, such as happens frequently with Bitcoin whenever its price approaches a sum that is evenly divisible by $10,000, for example. This point is known as resistance.

This regular occurrence is evidence that human traders are susceptible to emotional influence and frequently turn to shortcuts. If a specific price point is achieved for Bitcoin, there will undoubtedly be a flurry of market activity and expectations.

MOVING AVERAGES

Traders frequently smooth out this data to produce a single visual line representation known as the "moving average" using a market history of support/resistance levels and the associated upward/downward trendlines.

The moving average does a good job of following the peaks of resistance during a downward trend as well as the bottom support levels in an upward trend. A good indicator of short-term momentum is provided by the moving average when trading volume is taken into consideration.

CHART PATTERNS

The market can be charted in a variety of ways to look for patterns. The "candlestick" is one of the most popular visual depictions of market price activity. These candlestick patterns offer traders a kind of visual language to forecast potential trends.

Candlestick charts were developed in Japan in the 1700s as a technique to gauge how traders' emotions have a significant impact on price action in addition to pure supply-and-demand economics. Since it can include more information than the more straightforward line or bar charts, this market representation is one of the most popular among traders. There are four price points on a candlestick chart: open, close, high, and low.

What does this have to do with trading cryptocurrencies? Because of their rectangular design and the lines above and/or below that resemble a wick, they are known as candlesticks. Depending on the candle's color, the price opened or closed at the widest part of the candle. The price range in which an asset is traded during the course of the candlestick's predetermined period is represented by the wicks. Depending on the timeline chosen, candlesticks can represent various timespans, from one minute to one day and beyond, and exhibit various patterns.

TWELVE
STRUCTURE AND STRATEGIES OF CRYPTO TRADING

> *Bitcoin is here to stay. There would be a hacker uproar against anyone who attempted to take credit for the patent of cryptocurrency. And I wouldn't want to be on the receiving end of hacker fury.*
>
> ADAM DRAPER

STRUCTURE OF A TRADE

A buyer and a seller participate in a cryptocurrency transaction. Someone will always benefit more from a trade as there are two competing sides—a purchase and a sale. As a result, trading is by its very nature a zero-sum game in which both winners and losers exist. Basic knowledge of how the bitcoin markets function can be used to reduce potential losses and maximize gains.

When a buyer and seller agree on a price, the trade is carried out (via an exchange), and the asset's market value is established. The majority of the time, purchasers set Cryptocurrency prices often increase when there are more buy orders than sell orders, since there is greater demand for the asset. On the other hand, when there are more sellers than buyers, the price drops. Buys and sales are typically represented in distinct colors in exchange interfaces. This is done to quickly inform the trader about the market's condition at any particular time.

You may be familiar with the trading maxim, "Buy low, sell high." The adage does provide a fundamental illustration of the incentives of buyers and sellers in a marketplace, but it can be challenging to navigate because high and low prices might be relative. Simply put, you want to spend as little money as you can while making a transaction. If you want to sell anything, you want to get the biggest return on your investment. Although this is typically sound advice to abide by, there is the additional consideration of desiring versus shorting assets.

Going long on an asset (longing) means purchasing an asset and making money off of the asset's rising price movement. Contrarily, selling an asset with the goal to buy it back when its value drops below the level at which you sold it in order to profit from a price decline is known as shorting an asset. However, shorting entails the sale of borrowed assets that will be repaid later and is a little bit more difficult than this basic explanation. Later, these would be covered in more detail.

TRADING STRATEGY

Simply put, a trading strategy is a plan you adhere to when placing trades. Each trading strategy will mostly depend on the trader's profile and preferences because there is no one right way to do it. Regardless of how you trade, making a plan is essential because it specifies your objectives and can stop you from deviating from your route because of emotion. Normally, you should choose what you're trading, how you're going to trade it, and the entry and exit points.

There are four active trading techniques that are frequently used in the market. The act of confidently buying and selling while taking into account short-term market trends and profiting from the market's volatility is referred to as an "active trading strategy." The majority of experts think that long-term investment methods that involve buying and holding assets change with active trading tactics. Scalping, day trading, swing trading, and position trading are the four strategies, and they are described below:

DIFFERENT TYPES OF TRADING STRATEGIES

Day Trading

The strategy of day trading entails taking and closing trades on the same day. The phrase is derived from historical marketplaces, which only operate during specific hours of the day. Day traders are not expected to hold any open positions outside of certain times.

You undoubtedly already know that there are no set hours for starting or closing cryptocurrency markets. Every day of the year, you can trade all hours of the day. However, day trading typically refers to a trading strategy in which the trader enters and exits positions within a 24-hour period when used in relation to cryptocurrencies.

You'll frequently use technical analysis in day trading to choose which assets to trade. You can decide to trade a variety of assets to attempt to increase your returns because the earnings in such a short time can be rather small. However, some people might just exchange one pair for a long time. Clearly, this is a very active trading approach. Although it includes a substantial level of risk, it may be quite lucrative. Day trading is therefore typically more suitable for seasoned traders.

Swing Trading

Swing trading uses a longer time horizon than day trading; positions are typically held for a few days to a few months. The goal is still to profit from market trends. Finding an item that appears inexpensive and has the potential to appreciate in value will frequently be your objective. If you wanted to make money, you would buy this asset and sell it when its value increased. Alternately, you may try to identify assets that are overpriced and are likely to lose value. Then, in the event that you wanted to repurchase them, you could sell some of them for a high price.

Many swing traders employ technical analysis, just like day traders. Fundamental analysis may be more useful for longer-term investments due to their longer-term strategy. Swing trading is usually a more approachable strategy for new traders, mostly because it is less stressful than frantic day trading. In contrast to the latter, which demands quick decisions and prolonged screen time, swing trading gives you the freedom to take your time.

Position Trading

Trading positions (or trends) is a long-term tactic. Traders buy assets to hold for a long time (generally measured in months). They intend to turn a profit by reselling those assets in the future for more money.

The reasoning behind the trade is what separates position

trades from long-term swing trades. Position traders try to profit from the market's overall direction by focusing on patterns that can be seen over long time frames. On the other hand, swing traders generally try to forecast "swings" in the market that don't always correspond with the larger trend.

Position traders frequently choose fundamental analysis, merely because their desire for time allows them to observe fundamental events unfold. But that doesn't mean technical analysis isn't employed. The use of technical indicators can warn position traders of the likelihood of a trend reversal even while they operate on the premise that the trend will continue.

Position trading is a great approach for beginners, just as swing trading. Once more, the lengthy time horizon offers them plenty of time to think things through before making a choice.

Scalping

Scalping occurs over the shortest time spans of all the methods mentioned. Scalpers generally join and exit positions quickly, trying to take advantage of slight price changes (or even seconds). They typically employ technical analysis to try to forecast price fluctuations and take advantage of the bid-ask spread and other inefficiencies to profit. Due to the short time frames, scalping trades frequently provide tiny profits, typically less than 1%. However, since scalping is a game of numbers, a series of little profits can pile up over time.

Scalping is by no means a beginner's strategy. An in-depth understanding of the markets, the platforms you're trading on, and technical analysis are vital to success. That said, for traders that know what they're doing, identifying the right patterns and taking advantage of short-term fluctuations can be highly profitable.

OTHER TYPES OF CRYPTO TRADING STRATEGIES

Buy and Hold

Unsurprisingly, the "buy and hold" strategy entails purchasing and holding an asset. Investors buy the asset and then leave it alone for a long time, regardless of the state of the market. HODLing, which generally refers to investors who prefer to purchase and hold for years instead of actively trading, is a good example of this in the cryptocurrency market.

For those who prefer "hands-off" investing, this can be a beneficial strategy because they won't have to worry about short-term swings or capital gains taxes. On the other hand, it calls on the investor to exercise patience and makes the assumption that the asset won't become completely worthless.

Index Trading

One could think of index investing as a type of "buy and keep." As the name suggests, the investor's goal is to make money off the movement of assets inside a particular index. They could achieve this by investing in an index fund or making their own independent purchases of the assets. Once more, this is a passive tactic. Diversification across a variety of assets can also be advantageous for people without the strain of active trading.

Paper Trading

Any method could be used in paper trading, but the trader is merely acting out the purchase and sale of assets. This is an option you might take into consideration as a novice trader (or even as an expert trader) to test your abilities without risking any of your own money.

For instance, you might believe you've found a reliable method for predicting Bitcoin price declines and want to try making money off of them before they happen. However, you can decide to paper trade before putting all of your money in danger. This can be accomplished by simply noting the price when you "open" your short position and once more when you shut it. You could also use a simulator that looks like common trading interfaces.

The biggest advantage of paper trading is that you may experiment with different techniques without risking your own money. With no risk, you can simulate how your actions would have gone. Of course, you must be conscious that paper trading simply provides you with a distorted view of the real world. When your money is at stake, it's difficult to duplicate the true emotions you feel. If you don't account for them for certain platforms, paper trading without a real-world simulator could also offer you a false impression of associated costs and fees.

Long Position

A long position (or just long) is when you purchase an asset in the hope that its value will increase. Long positions can be applied to virtually any asset class or market type, however, they are most frequently utilized in the context of derivatives products or forex. A long position also includes purchasing an asset on the spot market with the expectation that its value will rise.

The most popular method of investing, especially for those who are just starting out, is going long on a crypto asset. The underlying asset will improve in value, which is the premise of long-term trading strategies like purchase and hold. In this view, buying and holding is just holding onto a position for a long time.

Being long, however, doesn't always imply that the trader

anticipates profiting from a price increase. Using leveraged tokens as an illustration. BTCDOWN and the cost of bitcoin are negatively connected. BTCDOWN's cost decreases when the price of bitcoin rises. The cost of BTCDOWN increases when the price of Bitcoin decreases. So, taking a long position in BTCDOWN is equivalent to expecting a decline in the price of bitcoin.

Shorting

A short position (or short) is when you sell a cryptocurrency asset with the goal of buying it again at a loss in the future. Margin trading and shorting are closely related because the latter can use borrowed assets. It is, however, very frequently employed in the futures market and is possible with a straightforward spot position. How then does "shorting" operate?

Shorting on-the-spot markets is very straightforward. Assume you already hold Bitcoin and that you anticipate a decline in its value. You exchange your BTC for USD with the intention of repurchasing it at a reduced cost. Since you're selling high to rebuy lower in this situation, you're essentially taking a short position on Bitcoin.

Simple enough. But what about using borrowed money to short? Let's check how that functions.

You take out a loan against a resource that you anticipate losing value, like a stock or a cryptocurrency. You sell it right away. You must buy back the same quantity of the asset that you borrowed if the trade is successful and the asset's price falls. You make money from the price difference between the original selling price and the price you paid to repurchase the assets while also returning the borrowed assets (together with interest).

What does shorting Bitcoin with borrowed money look like then? Let's examine a case in point. To borrow 1 BTC, we put up the necessary collateral, and we then sell it for $10,000 right away. We currently have $20,000. Suppose the cost drops to $16,000 instead. We purchase 1 BTC and use it to pay off our debt of 1 BTC plus interest. Our profit is $4,000 because we sold Bitcoin for $20,000 initially and now bought it for $16,000 instead (minus the interest payment and trading fees).

THIRTEEN
HOW TO START TRADING CRYPTOCURRENCIES

> *Bitcoin actually has the balance and incentives center, and that is why it is starting to take off.*
>
> JULIAN ASSANGE

You require trading capital before you can begin trading cryptocurrencies. It can drastically harm your life if you start trading with money you can't lose and don't have any savings. Trading is difficult; the vast majority of new traders experience losses. The money you set aside for trading may go quickly, and you might never be able to make up for your losses. It is advised to test the waters by beginning with modest amounts.

Your overall trading approach is another thing you should consider. When it comes to making money in the financial markets, there are several options available. You can select from a wide range of tactics to reach your financial objectives, depending on the amount of time and effort you are willing to invest in this endeavor.

Finally, let me make another point. When trading is not their primary source of income, many traders perform at their best. The emotional strain is lighter in this sense than if their daily survival were at stake. Successful traders have the ability to eliminate emotion, but doing so is far more difficult when one's livelihood is on the line. As a result, you could consider trading and investing as a side business, especially when you're first getting started. Also, keep in mind that you should start small in order to learn and practice. It could be wise to research cryptocurrency-based passive income opportunities.

A BEGINNER'S GUIDE TO CRYPTOCURRENCY TRADING

Finding a reputable cryptocurrency trading platform and setting up an account are the initial steps in cryptocurrency trading. When it comes to trading cryptocurrencies, individual cryptocurrency traders have various needs and objectives. Fortunately, there are many different trading platforms available online. Before selecting a platform, there are numerous things to take into account, including security, usability, the number of supported assets, and many more.

The next step is to register an account once a trustworthy platform has been chosen. The majority of platforms will provide you with a registration form to fill out. To register, you must first enter a working email address, then pick a secure password, and finally click Register. The next step is for you to confirm your account; a code will be sent to your email address along with the email.

The next step is to deposit your initial capital and start trading cryptocurrencies after the verification process has been successful. Money can be deposited using a number of methods, including credit/debit cards, Skrill, bank transfers, etc.

Cryptocurrency trading may seem easy. However, a variety of circumstances play a part in determining your level of success. Cryptocurrency trading is a wealth-building and income-generating strategy that calls on discipline, patience, and expertise rather than being a get-rich-quick gimmick.

CONSIDERATIONS FOR TRADING CRYPTOCURRENCIES

1. Trading journal

Your trading activities are recorded in a trading log. Do you need to keep one? Probably! A straightforward Excel spreadsheet or a paid service are also options.

Some traders believe that maintaining a trading notebook is crucial to becoming consistently profitable, particularly when it comes to more aggressive trading. After all, how can you determine your strengths and limitations if you don't record your trading activities? You wouldn't have a clear understanding of your results without a trading journal.

Remember that biases can significantly influence your trading decisions and that keeping a trading record can help you reduce some of them. How? Well, the facts speak for themselves. If everything boils down to numbers when it comes to trading success, and if you're not doing anything well, it will show. You may track which trading techniques work the best by methodically keeping a trading notebook.

2. Calculating Position Size in Trading

Risk management is among the most crucial components of trading. In fact, some traders contend that it is the most crucial factor. This is why using a consistent formula to determine the size of your positions is essential. Here is how the math works.

You must first decide how much of your account you are willing to put at risk with each deal. Let's assume that this is 1%. Does this imply that you only invest 1% of your account when entering positions? No, it just implies that you won't lose more than 1% of your account if your stop-loss is hit.

It might seem like too little, but this is to protect your account from a few unavoidable disastrous deals. Therefore, once this is established, you must choose the location of your stop-loss. Depending on the particulars of the trade proposal, you do this for each individual trade. Let's say you've decided to set your stop-loss 5 percent from the point when you entered the trade. This indicates that you should lose exactly 1% of your account when your stop-loss is reached and you exit 5 percent from your entry. Let's imagine our account has a balance of $1,000 USDT. With each trade, we take a 1% risk. The distance from our entry to our stop-loss is 5%. What size of a position should we use?

1000*0.01/0.05=200

If we want to only lose 10 USDT, which is 1% of our account, we should enter a 200 USDT position.

3. Online Trading Software

A fundamental component of any technical analyst's trading toolset is chart analysis. What is the ideal place to do that, though? There are many other vendors of online charting software on the market, and they all provide various advantages. However, you will typically need to pay a monthly subscription fee. Coinigy, TradingLite, Exocharts, and Tensorcharts are some platforms that specialize in cryptocurrency trading.

4. Paid Group for Trading

There is a wealth of excellent free trading knowledge available, so why not take advantage of it? Additionally, it is beneficial to practice trading independently so you can learn from your blunders and discover what suits you and your trading style the best.

A legitimate learning tool may be joining a paid organization, but beware of fraud and false advertising. As a matter of fact, it's really simple to fabricate trading results in order to get followers for a premium service. It's also important to consider the initial motivations behind a successful trader's decision to launch a paid group. A little extra money is always great, but if they are already doing so well, why would they need to charge so much for it?

Having said that, some prosperous traders operate premium paid communities with extra features like exclusive market data. Just be extra cautious about who you hand over your cash to, as the bulk of paid trading organizations seek to take advantage of inexperienced investors.

5. Understanding Pump and Dump (P&D)

A pump and dump scheme includes inflating an asset's price using fake information. The offenders sell ("dump") their cheaply purchased bags at a much higher price once the price has increased significantly.

The cryptocurrency markets are rife with pump-and-dump operations, particularly during bull periods. These times see a large influx of novice investors, who are easy to take advantage of. Due to the low liquidity of these marketplaces, this form of fraud is more prevalent with smaller market capitalization cryptocurrencies because it is often simpler to inflate their prices.

Private "pump and dump groups" frequently run pump and dump schemes, promising new members quick returns (usually in exchange for a fee). But typically, individuals that join are used by a far smaller group of people who have already established themselves. People who are found guilty of assisting pump and dump schemes in the legacy markets face severe fines.

6. Cryptocurrency Airdrops

Maybe, but exercise extreme caution! A creative technique to reach a broad audience with cryptocurrency is through airdrops. An airdrop can be a wonderful approach to prevent a cryptocurrency from becoming centralized in the possession of a small number of holders. For a robust, decentralized network, a varied group of holders is essential. There is no such thing as a free lunch, though. Well, occasionally, if you're extremely fortunate, there might be! The proponents of the airdrop will typically try to take advantage of you directly or will demand payment in exchange, however, this is not always the case.

Who will ask for what? Your personal information is one of the "assets" that are most frequently requested in exchange for an airdrop. Is a highly speculative cryptocurrency worth $10–$50 in exchange for your personal information? Your decision, but there might be better methods to supplement your income without jeopardizing your privacy or personal information. Because of this, you should exercise extreme caution when considering participating in cryptocurrency airdrops.

OTHER THINGS TO UNDERSTAND BEFORE TRADING CRYPTOCURRENCIES

1. Portfolio Management

The formation and administration of a group of investments is the focus of portfolio management. A collection of assets, the portfolio itself could include everything from Beanie Babies to real estate. It will most likely contain some combination of Bitcoin and other virtual currency and tokens if you just trade cryptocurrencies. The first thing you should do is think about your expectations for the portfolio. Are you searching for a portfolio of assets that will be largely insulated from volatility, or are you looking for something riskier that could result in quicker returns?

It is really advantageous to give your portfolio management some thought. Some people might favor a passive strategy, in which your investments are made and then left alone. Others can adopt an active strategy in which they consistently buy and sell assets in an effort to generate profits.

2. Risk Management

The control of risk is another important component of trading. Knowing how much you are willing to lose on cryptocurrency trading if it goes against you is crucial before you join a trade. This may depend on a variety of elements, including your trading money. For instance, a trader could only want to risk losing 1% of their whole trading capital overall or each trade.

Simply put, trading is a risky activity in and of itself. Any future market action cannot be predicted with accuracy. In the end, it's crucial to make your own decisions based on the material at hand and your own judgment, as well as to make sure you have received the appropriate education.

Additionally, based on tastes, personalities, trading capital, risk tolerance, etc., trading techniques can vary greatly from person to person. Trading entails a great deal of responsibility. Before choosing to trade, everyone considering it must assess their own circumstances.

Trading success depends on effective risk management. This starts with determining the categories of risk you might experience:

Market Risk: This is the possibility of financial losses brought on by the asset's depreciation.

Liquidity Risk: This is the possibility of losses due to illiquid markets, where it may be difficult to sell your assets.

Operational Risk: This is the possibility of suffering losses as a result of operational errors. These could result from employee fraud, hardware or software malfunctions, or human error.

Systemic Risk: This is the possibility of losses brought on by key firms in the sector you operate in failing, which has an effect on all companies there. The demise of Lehman Brothers had a ripple effect on global financial systems, much like it did in 2008.

As you can see, identifying risks starts with the assets in your portfolio, but for it to be effective, it needs to take into account both internal and external elements. The next step is to evaluate these hazards. How frequently are you likely to come across them? Just how bad are they?

You can rank the risks and come up with suitable strategies and actions by balancing the risks and determining their potential impact on your portfolio. For instance, market risk can be reduced by using stop-losses, and systemic risk can be reduced by diversifying investments.

3. Crypto Asset Allocation and Diversification

The terms "diversification" and "allocation of crypto assets" are frequently used interchangeably. The maxim "don't put all your eggs in one basket" may be familiar to you. Putting all of your financial eggs in one basket provides a single point of failure for you. You run the same danger if you put all of your savings into one asset. You would instantly lose your money if the asset in question was the stock of a certain firm, and that company later went bankrupt.

This applies to asset classes as well as to individual assets. You would anticipate that every stock you own will decrease in value in the event of a financial crisis. This is due to their strong correlation, which means that they all frequently exhibit the same pattern.

Simply stocking your portfolio with dozens of various digital currencies is not good diversification. Think about a scenario in which governments all around the world decide to outlaw cryptocurrency or quantum computers and manage to crack the public-key cryptography protocols we employ. All digital assets would be significantly impacted by either of these events. They belong to the same asset class as stocks.

Ideally, you should distribute your riches among several social classes. This will prevent the performance of one investment from negatively affecting the other investments in your portfolio. Harry Markowitz, a Nobel Prize winner, developed the Modern Portfolio Theory to do this (MPT). The theory essentially argues that integrating uncorrelated assets will reduce the volatility and risk involved with investments in a portfolio.

FOURTEEN
BECOMING A SUCCESSFUL CRYPTO TRADER

> *I see Bitcoin as ultimately becoming a reserve currency for banks, playing much the same role as gold did in the early days of banking. Banks could issue digital cash with greater anonymity and lighter weight, more efficient transactions.*
>
> HAL FINNEY

What distinguishes profitable cryptocurrency traders from the rest? What's more, how can you position yourself right now to become the best cryptocurrency trader you can be? In this chapter, we'll take a look at how to start trading cryptocurrencies successfully.

A crypto trader's ultimate purpose is to profit from short-term changes in cryptocurrency market values, which is a basic definition of "who is a crypto trader?". A cryptocurrency trader can concentrate on just one coin and pairing, such as the well-known BTCUSD Bitcoin pairings (or BTCEUR). They might also concentrate on several significant coins and, consequently, pairings, such as Bitcoin and Ethereum paired with either USD or EUR.

You may have heard the term "alts," which stands for alternative cryptocurrencies. Alts are typically thought of as smaller cryptocurrencies, and their market capitalization reflects that. Some cryptocurrency traders might simply pay attention to altcoins and make no effort to learn about the major cryptocurrencies. None of the aforementioned situations are inherently "bad," but finding the best course of action for your own circumstances, level of risk tolerance, and overall objectives are important.

It's important to briefly discuss the two scenarios you must take into account when researching how to become a crypto trader:

1. Buy and Sell Crypto on Exchanges

The cryptocurrency of your choice can be purchased straight from a crypto exchange, meaning you now have ownership of the coin's underlying asset. There are benefits to this strategy, but they are more pertinent when you wish to hold the cryptocurrency for a long time rather than use it for short-term trading.

Directly purchasing and holding cryptocurrencies on an exchange carries some risk because these platforms are susceptible to hacking, frequently (but not always) unregulated, and charge fees for both purchases and sales.

In order to use this option, the trader must deposit the entire position's value and keep the cryptocurrency in a secure wallet until they are prepared to sell it for a profit or loss (it is never recommended to store crypto directly in the exchange—another reason why this option is suited for a long-term strategy). This choice is comparable to an investor purchasing a tangible item, such as stock in a publicly listed corporation, and holding it for an extended period of time with the anticipation that its value would increase. However, given the long-term price volatility of cryptocurrencies, many traders and investors favor short-term trading (compared to long-term investment).

2. Trade Crypto CFDs

Trading cryptocurrency CFDs with a regulated broker is your secondary option; this is preferable if your investment horizon is limited (which is really the only viable option for trading, in the first place). With leverage, this category of crypto CFD traders simply needs to deposit a small portion of the total value of the position. In the article titled "What is Leverage in Trading?" you can read more about the advantages and hazards of leverage.

Cryptocurrency CFD traders can also "short" or "sell" cryptocurrency CFDs, which lets them make money when the market goes down. Given the upward and downward trends in the Bitcoin vs. US dollar chart above, employing CFDs might be a wise course of action.

Of course, there are also drawbacks to CFD trading in general. Market fluctuations that are broad and sudden put your money in danger and need to be watched carefully. Due to the frequent changes in market circumstances and the potential for the illiquidity of current contracts, liquidity risks must also be taken into account when trading CFDs.

Always using a sample account to test the markets is a good first step. Using a demo trading account, crypto CFD traders can test their trading theories and ideas in a risk-free virtual trading environment. As a result, they are able to trade on various cryptocurrency CFDs without needing to use real money.

Knowing which tools, trading techniques, and investment products are best for your particular goals is a crucial part of learning how to trade cryptocurrencies.

Trading cryptocurrency CFDs has greater advantages over purchasing cryptocurrency through an exchange in the two alternatives discussed above. This disparity is only one of many to take into account. Let's look at some additional ideas to think about when learning how to trade cryptocurrencies.

PROFITABILITY OF CRYPTO TRADING

Given the significant volatility that is constant in this market sector, trading bitcoin CFDs carries risk (as do all trading products). Trading bitcoin CFDs, however, can be quite successful provided you have a well-coordinated trading plan. As they say, great risk can lead to a high return.

The numbers speak for themselves; Bitcoin has so far surpassed every other marketable asset in 2021, making it the best-performing asset of the year. You have a chance to succeed as a crypto CFD trader if you are willing to do your research, develop a sound plan, and know what tools will be most helpful to you.

Naturally, it is challenging to predict with accuracy how much profit full- or part-time crypto traders make. Many people who trade cryptocurrency CFDs do so to expand their portfolio and reinvest the gain into their upcoming actions. Therefore, a lot of CFD traders that deal in cryptocurrency might not be doing so for a living. Nevertheless, the number of people abandoning their jobs to trade cryptocurrency is undoubtedly on the rise, with Millennials leading the charge.

Unfortunately, there isn't yet enough publicly available data to provide you with a realistic range of salaries for full-time cryptocurrency traders.

PASSIVE VS. ACTIVE INVESTING IN CRYPTOCURRENCIES

When comparing cryptocurrency investment strategies to more established asset classes like equities investments, it is helpful to think of cryptocurrencies as a new asset class. For instance, the advantages of passive vs. active investing are one of the most hotly debated issues in the stock investment industry. The discussion of the relative pros and hazards of the two approaches would make a good dissertation and is outside the purview of this book. But in general, passive investment is more long-term and calls for a "buy-and-hold" mindset, whereas active investing is more hands-on.

In the case of equities investment, for instance, you would have to choose between purchasing a broadly diversified fund, such as an S&P 500 index fund, and an actively managed fund where the fund manager makes stock selections. As an alternative, you might actively manage the portfolio yourself by selecting and tracking your own stocks. The cryptocurrency industry uses the same strategies, but many of the products are still in the early stages of development.

Active Investing

Utilizing a cryptocurrency exchange is by far the most common way to trade cryptocurrencies. Websites known as cryptocurrency exchanges allow users to purchase, sell, or swap cryptocurrencies for fiat money or other forms of digital money. Most cryptocurrency exchanges allow users to trade one cryptocurrency for another, therefore it is possible to buy one cryptocurrency with another without using fiat money (like US Dollars). The biggest exchanges, which transact more than $100 million (or its equivalent) each day, are Poloniex, Bitfinex, Kraken, and GDAX.

Even so, some exchanges allow you to fund your account using fiat money through a wire transfer. Even the purchase of cryptocurrency using a credit card is possible on some exchanges, albeit with strict limits and expensive fees (e.g., 3.99% at Coinbase, the biggest US-based exchange). Only a few well-known cryptocurrencies, such as Bitcoin, Bitcoin Cash, Ether, and Litecoin, are typically accepted on exchanges that take fiat payments. You can then use these cryptocurrencies to buy other, less well-known ones. You can use this website to find out which exchanges can be accessed from a particular nation or which accepts a particular form of payment.

Exchanges vary in significant ways as well. One is the Know-Your-Client (KYC) rules, which may or may not force exchanges to request a particular amount of user information. The majority of exchanges nowadays, and undoubtedly those that trade in fiat currency, need user identification and evidence of residency. Additionally, exchange-specific fees vary but typically range from 0 to 0.5%. Some exchanges also provide value-added services, like Coinbase's Vault, which stores your currencies in a supposedly more safe location when you aren't exchanging them right away. Lastly, while this is a matter of personal opinion, certain user interfaces are "cleaner" while others are "busier."

Let's utilize a real-world illustration. Imagine you used Coinbase to purchase BTC using fiat currency and now you want to purchase NEO, which is not traded on Coinbase. Find a trading platform for NEO, such as Binance, and create an account there first. You will be given an address (also known as a "public key") by Binance so that you can send bitcoins from Coinbase to your Binance account. You can use the BTC to buy NEO on Binance after it appears in your Binance account.

One more point: It is crucial to compare prices because it is not unusual to observe sizable pricing discrepancies between exchanges. Additionally, if you reside in a nation with unique conditions like currency restrictions or an unusual political climate, you can find that the local BTC price is markedly higher than the average worldwide.

The search for a counterparty (buyer or seller) on your own is another "conventional" method. If you want to send or receive cryptocurrency, you will need a wallet. If you wanted to buy some Bitcoin for fiat, you would provide the seller with your wallet's public key and then pay with fiat once the Bitcoin had arrived in your wallet. Localbitcoins.com is a well-known way of conducting these peer-to-peer transactions. You should obviously carry out such transactions in a public, secure setting, possibly during a meetup of a nearby bitcoin group (which you can find via sites like meetup.com).

Selling: The same channels you used for buying are open when you're ready to sell some or all of your coins. In other words, you can sell at an ATM, directly to a customer, or even on an exchange.

You will be able to exchange cryptocurrencies for fiat money immediately on some exchanges, just like when you buy them. However, in other circumstances involving lesser cryptocurrencies, you will need to go through the extra step of exchanging your cryptocurrencies for a "mainstream" cryptocurrency like BTC or Ether, which you can then exchange for fiat money, in order to obtain it.

Obviously, this will result in two transactions, double the fees, and a longer time of exposure to market risk. It's crucial to keep in mind that liquidity may not be available exactly when you need it in this still-evolving market, especially when prices are moving quickly. This is especially true when crypto exchanges are down. Debit cards are another way to "sell," and you may use them to withdraw money from your virtual wallet and make purchases.

Passive Investing

Here are a few products you may use to expose passive investments to cryptocurrencies.

Vehicles Tracking One Currency: Purchasing a vehicle that tracks a single, highly liquid cryptocurrency is one strategy. The few passive products in use today track Bitcoin (BTC), the original cryptocurrency that has long dominated the market. These include the Bitcoin Investment Trust (GBTC) from Grayscale Investment, the Bitcoin Tracker One ETN, and the Bitcoin certificate offered by Vontobel, a private bank in Switzerland. For instance, since its May 2015 introduction, GBTC has been traded on the US over-the-counter market. It is the biggest and most actively traded fund in the cryptocurrency market with $2.6 billion in total assets as of this writing. Since the fund's founding, its value has increased by 4,300%.

Although it is passively managed and aims to mimic the movement of a BTC exchange-traded fund (ETF), its application for ETF registration has not yet been accepted by the SEC. The CBOE and the NYSE are two additional parties that have registered to start ETFs.

One benefit of these products is that you might be able to purchase them using your current brokerage account because they are listed on "normal" exchanges, such as Nasdaq Nordic for the Bitcoin Tracker One. Additionally, you don't need to be concerned with practical matters like how to store, buy, or sell your cryptocurrency.

They can be trading over their actual net asset value, which is a drawback. For instance, because GBTC is the only BTC trust of its sort, the price of GTBC has frequently increased well beyond the value of the underlying BTC! Another drawback is that, other than the Ethereum Tracker One ETN, Grayscale's Ethereum Classic Investing Trust, and Zcash Investment Trust, there aren't many passive investment choices for cryptocurrencies other than Bitcoin (BTC).

Vehicles Tracking Multiple Currencies: A financial instrument that tracks multiple cryptocurrencies takes things a step further. For this goal, numerous products are now being developed. Several should be introduced in 2018, including the Crypto Market Index Fund by the Swiss business Crypto Finance AG. In its first year, the fund hopes to raise $113 million in AUM, with a three-year end goal of $3.4 billion. Investor commitment to the fund stood at $11.3 million as of the middle of 2017, with an additional $11.3 million in transition. The fund will have a wide range of investments, which will reduce volatility while preserving the "rapid growth" advantages of new cryptocurrencies.

Futures: Bitcoin futures are a new, widely-publicized way to gain exposure to BTC. Depending on the prices that speculators "wager" BTC will reach in the future, buyers and sellers are required under bitcoin futures contracts to buy or sell BTC. By enabling investors to bet on the price of BTC without actually owning it, these futures are intended to reduce price volatility. There are two primary effects: One of the reasons is that, despite the fact that Bitcoin is mostly uncontrolled, BTC futures can be traded on regulated exchanges, allaying some investors' fears about market regulation. Second, these futures would enable investors to engage in countries like Bolivia and Bangladesh where trading in bitcoin is outlawed by law.

In December 2017, BTC futures trading launched on CBOE and CME. In 2018, it will launch on NASDAQ. Be aware that the margin requirements—over 40% on the long side and over 100% on the short side—are quite high. Note that cash-settled futures and exchange-traded notes (ETNs) won't help you if you want to utilize cryptocurrencies as a hedge against the collapse of the current fiat paper currency system because they don't provide you direct ownership of the underlying cryptocurrency. Futures are undoubtedly sophisticated financial products, so before utilizing them, you need to get the right knowledge and counsel.

THE BASICS ON HOW TO BECOME A CRYPTO TRADER

For each trader, success as a cryptocurrency trader will entail a different meaning. For some, it can mean turning a profit while trading on a live account using the 30-minute chart. For others, it can be turning a profit on bitcoin CFD shorting. The key to success, though, will be generating a profit on the money you put at risk. The knowledge and tools you utilize will have the biggest influence on your total success, just like in any business.

The following are the fundamentals that you should be

aware of in order to improve your chances of long-term success as a cryptocurrency trader:

Choose the Right Broker

You must first have a broker in order to execute transactions in order to be able to trade bitcoin CFDs, which comes as no surprise.

It might be difficult to select the "perfect" broker because there are so many possibilities and they are all vying for your business. The most crucial thing is to ensure that they are governed, ideally by several different governments. The highest standards of security and safety are guaranteed by the regulatory control of the numerous regulatory organizations.

Choose a Reliable Trading Platform

Your trading and charting software offers you the order tickets you need to place and manage your trades, as well as historical price charts of the asset you are trading.

Some people might use a separate charting platform from their brokerage platform. However, with the help of cutting-edge trading technology, you can combine your brokerage platform and charting platform into one location with the MetaTrader family of products.

Choose Your Crypto Trading Strategy

Making choices on whether to purchase, sell, or hold steady in a specific market is the essence of trading. A trading technique, or methodology, is considerably more likely to be used by traders who have sustained success over an extended period of time.

The usage of trading techniques can speed up the process of gathering information, such as when to trade and when not to, which timeframes to concentrate on, which technical indicators to employ, how to enter and exit, and so on. Naturally, the tools you employ will depend on the trading approach you select. The first step in learning how to trade cryptocurrencies is to establish this.

After all, using the long-term weekly chart for analysis may not be particularly helpful if your objective is to day trade cryptocurrency CFDs from the hourly chart, which entails buying and selling multiples throughout the day for short-term profits and closing out positions at the end of the day.

WHAT THE BEST CRYPTO TRADERS HAVE IN COMMON

It's crucial to keep in mind that trading is all about choosing whether to place a transaction or not, regardless of the market you are trading in or the strategy you decide to use. The majority of people dislike making snap judgments about their finances. In actuality, most people prefer to take their time—analyzing the information, conducting research, and so forth—before making a significant financial decision.

When it comes to trading, nothing is more crucial than what was just mentioned. This is especially true if you are studying to become a cryptocurrency trader. Successful cryptocurrency traders are aware of this and will optimize their trading environment to govern and control their decision-making. The following are just a few optimization techniques you could discover the most successful cryptocurrency traders using:

Defined Crypto Trading Style

As was covered in the previous part, choosing a trading style is crucial because it will determine how you make trading decisions and direct you to the data you need to analyze that is most appropriate for your objectives.

Research and Analysis

The finest trading decisions are often those that have required a substantial amount of prior research and analysis. Depending on how much importance you place on technical analysis and fundamental analysis, the type of research and analysis you conduct will vary.

A Happy Life Outside of the Markets

The caliber of your life determines how good your decisions will be. If you're feeling unhappy or regretful outside of the markets, those emotions will seep into your trading decisions. This is covered in more detail in my trading psychology tips.

Keep your risk moderate, account for the learning curve, and, most importantly, have pleasure in the process of discovering more about the markets and yourself.

Focus on Risk Relative to Reward

Since trading involves both winning and losing, it is a game of probabilities. A significant element of establishing and maintaining success as a cryptocurrency trader is risk management. One method of defending oneself against significant losses, for instance, is to use a stop loss.

RISKS INVOLVED IN TRADING CRYPTOCURRENCY

Trading on the cryptocurrency market carries a significant level of risk due to its high level of volatility. Before you begin trading, it's critical to comprehend the hazards involved, such as:

Volatility

Due to how unpredictable the cryptocurrency market is, prices can change dramatically in a short amount of time.

Cryptocurrency prices can fluctuate erratically based on fear and emotion rather than underlying fundamentals or technical trading patterns since there is no significant real-world usage for them.

Crashes

Huge crashes have occurred as a result of the bitcoin market's instability. For instance, in 2018 a total of nearly $700 billion was lost from the market capitalization of all cryptocurrencies due to a variety of problems, including:

- Cyber thefts
- Illegal initial coin offerings (ICOs)
- Hacks
- Exchange outages
- Loose to zero regulation
- Money laundering
- Tax evasion
- Excessive speculation

On bitcoin exchanges, there has been a long history of successful hacking efforts. This is obviously a good argument in favor of trading cryptocurrency CFDs rather than actual cryptocurrency on exchanges.

This includes the 2018 Coincheck hack in Japan, where more than $500 million worth of digital currency was taken, as well as the 2014 closure of the Japanese exchange Mt. Gox, which handled nearly 80% of all global Bitcoin transactions, and the loss of 850,000 bitcoins (worth roughly half a billion dollars!) from its virtual vaults.

It's important to keep in mind that when trading crypto, there is also a risk associated with the individual trader. Taking large, high-risk trading positions with the expectation of always winning is a surefire way to lose a lot of money. At the end of the day, each trader selects where to enter and exit the market as well as how much money to risk, therefore it's critical to have a sound trading strategy to account for these risks.

FIFTEEN
HOW TO TRADE CRYPTOCURRENCIES RESPONSIBLY

> *If you like gold, there are many reasons you should like Bitcoin.*
>
> CAMERON WINKLEVOSS

It's by no means simple to develop into a responsible crypto trader. It frequently requires a lot of patience, time, planning, and study. Nothing can stop you from trading cryptocurrency responsibly once you have started, and ultimately it becomes a regular part of your routine and a major priority. Planning and responsibility are two characteristics that set prudent traders apart from those who are not always cautious and thorough about their purchasing and selling selections. You can reduce many potential trading hazards by doing thorough planning. Planning is essentially what holds traders ultimately responsible for their actions.

IMPORTANCE OF PLANNING

Now that we are aware that long-term success depends on responsible trading, let's explore why preparation is crucial to becoming a trustworthy trader. As was covered in one of the earlier chapters, feelings, and movements in the cryptocurrency market are primarily driven by emotions. Therefore, maintaining emotional control and maintaining your composure is crucial.

When purchasing or selling cryptocurrency, trading responsibly should be your main goal. Planning ahead is key to trading responsibly. Making a trading plan can aid you later on by holding you responsible for your activities.

You can prevent emotions from influencing your trades by making decisions when your mind is clear. Additionally, you should think about conducting your own research, diversifying your portfolio, utilizing stop-limit orders, and avoiding FOMO wherever you can.

If you use leverage in your trading, be sure you are fully aware of the hazards. The Cooling-Off Period is one of the tools to provide you with more control over the volume of your trades. With this choice, you can lock your futures account for a specific amount of time.

Regardless of how much you trade, it's vital to be sure you're trading sensibly. You may lower needless risks and make sure you're only dealing with money you can afford to lose by following some easy advice and techniques. Some folks may find it simple to lose control. So that you can learn how to manage your trades more effectively, let's look at how to establish proper limitations and increase your total responsibility.

ETHICAL TRADING

Responsible cryptocurrency trading involves more than just keeping track of your purchases and sales. Instead of acting on your emotions when trading, you should be in control of your behavior. Additionally, you must accept responsibility and determine whether your trading activity is actually beneficial to you.

You can invest in or trade cryptocurrencies in a variety of ways. Alternatives like futures and margin trading are risky but can yield huge rewards through leverage. Some traders can find it challenging to handle things responsibly. A safer choice and one that may fit your risk tolerance better is purchasing cryptocurrency on the spot market and holding onto it.

The actions and attitudes that can result in irresponsible trading will be avoided by responsible traders. Recognizing when your decision-making may be negatively affected is a big component of trading cryptocurrency ethically. This ability does develop with time and expertise, and rookie traders frequently deal impulsively or rely solely on intuition. This should be avoided as much as possible.

TIPS TO HELP YOU TRADE CRYPTO RESPONSIBLY

In order to trade cryptocurrencies safely, you must control a number of different facets of your trading activity. The buy or sell button doesn't mark the beginning and conclusion of it. Try to include as many of the following ideas as you can into your daily activities. Even though it may seem like a lot of advice, it will help you develop your trading abilities.

1. Secure Your Wallet and Trading Account

Securing your account is the finest thing you can do before you even begin trading. Regardless of how carefully you prepare your transactions, they are useless if your money, account, or password are stolen. Utilizing two-factor authentication (2FA), making a strong password, and whitelisting withdrawal addresses are just a few of the methods available to accomplish this.

The same guidelines apply to your private key if you also utilize an external cryptocurrency wallet. Like your bank account information, you should never divulge your private key or seed phrase to a third party. You can choose from my list of suggested Binance Smart Chain wallets based on your needs and desired level of security. Extra money can be safely stored on a hardware wallet if you have the option to do so.

Since cryptocurrency is profitable, hackers are coming up with increasingly cunning ways to take your funds. Read on to find out how to use the following advice to protect your cryptocurrency wallet and personal information.

Two-Factor Authentication: This additional security measure ensures that only you can access your money. A username, password, and typically a security question are required as the two authentication methods.

Write Your Password or Wallet Somewhere Safe: You receive a 12-word seed phrase for each wallet that enables access to your trades. To prevent potential cyberattacks, we encourage you to write down your password physically (i.e. on a piece of paper) rather than saving it digitally.

Maintain Different Wallets: It is advisable to hold your assets on several distinct wallets since there is no restriction on the number of wallets you can have. Use one wallet for daily purchases and another for long-term investments, for instance. By using this technique, you may safeguard your portfolio and guard against account breaches.

Regularly Change Your Password: Everyone advises us to change our passwords frequently, but whether we actually do so is another matter. We strongly advise updating your wallet password every three months when it comes to protecting your hard-earned cryptocurrency.

2. Create a Trading Plan

The greatest method to ensure that your emotions don't affect your trade is to make a plan and follow it. This will prevent unexpected gains, losses, rumors, or FUD from influencing your choices. What then comprises a trading plan?

Your strategy should specify the types of transactions you wish to execute, the terms under which you will trade, and your trading goals. Your limitations will be based on your risk profile and trading approach. You should have a clear head when developing your trading strategy and be willing to stick to your decisions in the future. In your trading strategy, you could ask yourself:

- How diversified your portfolio is
- What your crypto asset allocation is
- When to stop trading (time, volume, etc.)
- What your maximum losses are
- What the products or assets you trade are
- How much leverage do you want to use if any at all
- What the entry and exit prices for specific trades are
- What the maximum investment amount as a percentage of total capital is

3. Use Stop-Limit Orders

Stop-limit orders are a simple way to get more control over your trading on Binance. Since cryptocurrency is so erratic, you can experience unforeseen losses if you can't spend all of your time in front of a screen. It's not a responsible method to trade to leave sizable sums of cryptocurrency exposed to volatility. Once you've established a trading strategy, using stop-limit orders to adhere to it is simple.

Imagine, for instance, that you bought 1 Bitcoin (BTC) for $15,000 (US dollars), and that Bitcoin is now worth $40,000. Make sure that you won't sell for less than $30,000 if the price drops. Your profit will be $15,000 as a result. You can create a sell stop-limit order to automate this.

The stop price is initially fixed at $32,000. Your limit order will be triggered at this price. The limit price is then set to $30,000, guaranteeing that your 1 BTC will sell for that amount or more if the stop price is achieved.

Your stop-limit order has the best probability of filling if there is a space between the stop price and the limit price. The market price can drop below your maximum price without satisfying your order if there isn't a gap.

Although a stop-limit order isn't always guaranteed to be filled, you will always receive the price you specified or better when it does.

4. Do Your Own Research

Even though many exchanges provide educational and research materials, this should only be the start of your investigation. By conducting your own research, you can confirm and verify any information you find. This recommendation applies to both using Decentralized Finance (DeFi) products and trading and investing in coins through exchanges. Your risk tolerance and what works for your portfolio are things that only you can determine. Make sure you have a solid knowledge of where you're putting your money before you start trading and investing.

5. Diversify Your Portfolio

Portfolio diversity should be covered in your trading plan if you choose to do so in order to lower your risk. It's often riskier to own just one or two assets in your portfolio. In order to diversify your holdings, you can invest in various assets across several asset classes.

You might start by deciding on your asset allocation in cryptocurrency. Your money could be divided across DeFi liquidity pools, staking, derivatives, stablecoins, and alternative currencies. You decrease your risk of suffering significant losses by limiting your exposure to a single crypto class. For instance, you might suffer a temporary loss from a liquidity pool in which you have invested but be able to make up for it by making stake gains. Following that, you can diversify within these various asset classes. Holding BUSD, USDT, and PAXG stablecoins would further lower the total risk of your portfolio. However, these are only instances. There are several ethical ways to organize your cryptocurrency holdings.

6. Avoid FOMO

For many traders, the fear of missing out (FOMO) is a prevalent emotion. You must be mindful of how it influences your behavior, though. Your limitations and trading strategies may be abandoned in favor of making snap decisions out of worry that you will miss out on a lucrative investment opportunity. As a result of having such easy access to information through the internet, social media, and other forms of communication, we are all vulnerable.

Online research and good investment options are there, but you should always be on the lookout for scams. Regardless of their true value, users with ulterior financial goals will promote their coins or initiatives. Scammers will use FOMO and influence traders' feelings. If you feel like you're missing out on an opportunity you've never heard of, spend some time thoroughly researching the venture before putting your money in danger.

Social Media: Rumors, misleading information, and scams can be found on Twitter, Telegram, Reddit, and other social networks. DYOR is a must at all times. Scammers may exploit your FOMO to steal your money, as many influencers are paid to promote projects and altcoins.

Gains: It can be tempting to become careless with your gains if you've been on a winning trend. Additionally, you could make poor choices if you have excessive confidence in your abilities. Even if you've made a sizable profit, this may make you feel more FOMO about potential "huge" investment prospects.

Losses: Your FOMO may intensify in an effort to make up for losses. Due to FOMO, you can even open a trade, close it after suffering losses, and then open it again. Both of these can result in considerably greater losses.

Gossip and Rumors: Learning about investment through other traders or the internet can make it look alluring. Rumors, financial advice, or suggestions for a well-liked cryptocurrency, however, should never replace thorough investigation and examination.

Volatility: Significant price swings in both directions

present business chances. It might be simple to get carried away when buying cryptocurrencies in the hopes that the price will rise or when shorting the market during a slump. A bearish market could also present a profitable investment opportunity, but you risk catching a falling knife.

7. Understand Leverage

It can be alluring to consider using margins or futures to borrow money in order to realize higher gains. However, because your losses are also increased, you run the risk of being liquidated and losing all of your capital quickly. If you stay inside your boundaries, liquidation isn't always awful. Trading responsibly, however, does not involve exceeding your expectations in terms of losses or financial risk. Make sure you fully comprehend how leverage functions before attempting to use it.

Leverage is sometimes represented as a multiplier, like 10x, which increases your starting capital by that amount by ten. You can trade with $100,000 using $10,000 leveraged 10x, and your initial investment is utilized to offset any losses. The exchange liquidates your stake when your capital is depleted.

Trading using leverage can be done recklessly. Because the risk is substantially larger, be sure to thoroughly research Coin-Margined Futures and USDT-Margined Futures. In order to promote responsible trading, Binance additionally safeguards new users by restricting their leverage.

8. Use a Cool-Off Period

Some exchanges allow you to manage the amount you trade in order to assist traders in using leverage responsibly. The cooling-off period can be used to maintain your trading strategy and guarantee that you only engage in trading within your means. You can choose to freeze your account for up to a month by turning on the functionality. The Cooling-Off Period cannot be turned off after it has started until the timer expires.

9. Practice Different Trading Strategies

The cryptocurrency market is unstable and constantly shifting. Therefore, starting to trade the same assets is the only way to truly grasp the market. Dummy accounts assist in practicing how the market functions in reality. Online, there are numerous fake accounts for various coins. Select the one that best suits your needs and practice it every day.

10. Update Your Knowledge About Cryptocurrency

Daily changes in the bitcoin market bring about new facets of the trade. You should keep up with current events if you want to succeed with investments. Cable news is a great source of trustworthy news, as are social media sites like Twitter, Facebook, and Telegram. To assure earnings, modify your investments in response to market developments.

11. Learn Trading Methods and Staking

The cryptocurrency market uses two different techniques for trading analysis. They comprise technical analysis as well as fundamental analysis. While fundamental analysis focuses on the current events that influence an asset's price, such as news events, technical analysis reveals the whole price history of security, such as bitcoin. The most effective way to increase revenues is to combine the two strategies. Always start staking your cryptocurrency to generate passive revenue. This is one of the simplest ways to profit long-term from cryptocurrency.

12. Embrace Mistakes

Trading cryptocurrencies is not a quick-rich scam. To succeed in trading, you need discipline, experience, and expertise. However, even experienced traders occasionally experience losses due to trading errors. Trading in cryptocurrencies might result in a loss of capital because they are unstable and dangerous. When it comes to becoming and remaining profitable, developing trading discipline and skills like risk management will go a long way. And keep trying even when you make mistakes. Learn from your errors.

SIXTEEN
GROWING YOUR WEALTH WITH CRYPTOCURRENCIES

> *You can't stop things like Bitcoin. It will be everywhere and the world will have to readjust. World governments will have to readjust.*
>
> JOHN MCAFEE

Everyone enters the cryptocurrency industry with the intention of making money, but not everyone succeeds. With the increase in crypto frauds, many people either give up along the route or fall victim to some form of trap.

Actually, aside from the apparent method of trading, there are quite a few additional ways to use cryptocurrencies to earn genuine income. As a result, I made the decision to investigate some of the tested methods for using cryptocurrencies to generate income. I discovered quite a few, but rest assured that you'll find them to be very impressive.

1. Investing

The long-term tactic of acquiring and retaining cryptographic assets for some time is called investing. A buy-and-hold strategy works effectively with most crypto assets. They have huge long-term growth potential but are somewhat volatile in the short term.

Finding longer-lasting, more stable assets is a requirement of the investing approach. Assets like Bitcoin and Ethereum are secure investments since they have a history of showing long-term price increases.

2. Trading

While trading aims to take advantage of short-term opportunities, investing is a long-term undertaking based on the buy-and-hold strategy. The cryptocurrency market is erratic. This implies that asset prices might change drastically over a short time, both up and down.

You need to possess the necessary technical and analytical abilities to succeed as a trader. To create precise forecasts about price increases and declines, you'll need to evaluate market charts on the performance of the listed assets.

Depending on whether you anticipate an increase or decline in an asset's price, you can trade by taking either a long or short position. This implies that you can earn whether the cryptocurrency market is bullish or bearish.

3. Staking and Lending

Staking is a method for confirming cryptocurrency transactions. You own coins if you are staking, but you do not use them. Instead, you secure the dollars in a digital wallet. Your coins are then used by a Proof of Stake network to verify transactions. You get rewarded for doing this. In a sense, you are lending the network coins. As a result, the network may continue to be secure and validate transactions. Your incentive is comparable to the interest that a bank would offer you on a credit balance.

The number of coins you have agreed to stake determines how many transaction validators are chosen by the Proof of Stake algorithm. Because of this, it uses a lot less energy than crypto mining and doesn't require expensive technology. Additionally, you have the option of lending coins to other investors and earning interest on that loan. Numerous platforms enable crypto financing.

4. Mining

In the same way, as the original pioneers did, you may make money with cryptocurrencies by mining them. Still, an essential part of the Proof of Work method is mining. It is the source of a cryptocurrency's value. A bitcoin miner receives new coins as payment. Technical know-how and initial investment in specialized hardware are required for mining. Mining is a subset of running a master node. It calls for knowledge as well as a sizable initial and ongoing expenditure.

5. Airdrops and Forks

To raise awareness, free tokens and airdrops are given out. To build a sizable user base for a project, an exchange might perform an airdrop. You can receive a free coin by participating in an airdrop, which you can then use to make purchases, investments, or trades.

A protocol upgrade or change that produces new currencies causes a blockchain to fork. Usually, you will receive free tokens on the new network if you have the currency on the original chain. This indicates that because you were in the correct position at the right moment, you received a free coin.

6. Buy and HODL

This is the most typical method of using cryptocurrency to make money. The majority of investors buy cryptocurrencies like Bitcoin, Litecoin, Ethereum, Ripple, and others and wait for their values to increase. They sell for a profit once their market prices increase.

For this investing strategy to work, you need to find assets that are both stable and volatile, so they can change in value quickly and give you consistent returns. Assets like Bitcoin and Ethereum have a history of maintaining consistent price variations; as a result, they can be viewed as secure investments in this sense. However, you are free to sell any item that you believe will increase in value; all you have to do is research every asset you buy before deciding to HODL it.

Additionally, investing in pricey assets is not necessary in order to benefit. Consider having a mix of all coins that have a promising future value and are not just well-liked in the exchanges. There are thousands of small altcoins that have reasonable price changes.

7. Earn Cryptocurrency Dividends

You can purchase cryptocurrencies and hold them for the dividend, did you know that? There are a few coins, nevertheless, that will pay you just for acquiring and holding their digital assets. The best part about these coins, especially when stored in a wallet, is that you don't even have to stake them.

COSS, CEFF, NEO, KUCOIN, and other coins are a few examples of those that distribute dividends. Not all of these coins, like traditional equities, are appropriate for your portfolio; you must study and choose those that appear to be consistent with your investing goals.

8. Run Cryptocurrency Master Nodes

A crypto master node is what? These are full nodes that encourage the various node operators to carry out their functions in running a blockchain. In other words, a master node is a bitcoin full node or digital wallet that keeps a running log of all transactions on a blockchain. Although the concept behind master nodes is quite complex, the following is a succinct explanation:

Running crypto master nodes is one of the most popular ways to make passive income in this industry. However, how exactly do you profit from this? Numerous cryptocurrencies compensate node operators for keeping an up-to-date log of their transactions on their native blockchains. Since the procedure is complicated and requires one to have a specific minimum amount of coins under their master nodes, cryptocurrency platforms prefer to pay master node operators to provide the service. DASH and PIVX are two examples of proof-of-stake cryptocurrencies with master nodes.

9. Day Trading

More than 80% of cryptocurrency investors think that day trading is the only practical method to make money in this industry, if not the only way. However, most of them are unaware that day trading entails more than merely keeping an item until its value increases; it is difficult to become a day trader, and having the necessary analytical and technical abilities is crucial.

The most challenging but, in my opinion, one of the most rewarding ways to make money with cryptocurrencies is to evaluate market charts on the performance of the listed assets. Any exchange today allows you to start day trading; all you have to do is sign up, purchase some assets, and evaluate.

You can also begin trading using an automated trading platform like bitcoin profit, which enables users to interpret signals sent out by trends on bitcoin and other cryptocurrencies and begin operating as a successful little trader. If you plan to day trade, you should think about becoming an expert in stock analysis, utilizing the technical and fundamental approaches, which are frequently employed to assess all traded assets.

10. Help with Microtasks for Cryptocurrency

You can work on little jobs for people or on bitcoin sites and earn money if you have additional time. The tasks can be very different; they could involve testing apps, watching advertisements, doing surveys, watching films, and more. Microtasks are available on websites like Bitcoin Rewards, Coinbucks, and Bituro.

11. Work for Cryptocurrency Companies

This is a typical method of making money in the industry. Anybody can work for a bitcoin business in any capacity; you could, for example, be a digital marketer, content creator, or web designer. All you have to do is determine their needs and demonstrate how your abilities can help them.

The nicest part of working with crypto platforms is that you'll probably do so remotely, giving you the freedom to do so in the comfort of your own home. Other than that, most crypto companies offer really appealing packages, so if you have the possibility to work with any trustworthy ones, seize the chance.

Here are a few instances of websites that accept digital payments.

- Coinality
- bitWAGE
- JobsforBitcoin
- Angle.co
- XBTFreelancer
- Coinworker

- 21.co

These sites pay their employees in cryptocurrencies, so your earnings may more than double in value in a matter of days, if not hours.

12. Crypto Arbitrage

Since the cryptocurrency industry is mostly unregulated, there are many differences in terms of asset valuation, product pricing, and other factors. The majority of exchanges set their own listing prices, which has helped to eliminate differences in asset volatility and liquidity. If carefully considered, buying from inexpensive sources and selling on exorbitant exchanges are two ways to profit from these price discrepancies. Arbitrage is essentially described in this manner.

If you put your act together, you can locate price spreads on several exchanges ranging from 5% to 30%. Consider registering on several sites and comparing asset prices to uncover any appreciable differences to profit from.

13. Cryptocurrency Faucets

Although they are not particularly well known, cryptocurrency faucets are a very effective way to make money. The most well-known ones are bitcoin faucets, which are essentially a reward system that functions as a website or application and provides incentives to eligible users in the form of Satoshi. A Satoshi is a reward given for completing a task, such as capture, or any other that may be necessary by the application or website. It is equal to one-hundredth of a millionth BTC.

The responsibilities could even take the form of enjoyable activities like playing games, watching films, or seeing particular advertisements. You receive a tiny amount of Bitcoin for each assignment you complete.

14. Create Cryptocurrency Content

One of the most efficient ways to reach out to current or potential customers during the last ten years is through content. The most effective way to launch new goods or services is through content.

Because most projects in the cryptocurrency industry are virtual, content marketing plays a significant role in this industry. Therefore, it might not be able to contact the target population through traditional marketing techniques. You can provide written material, infographics, or videos for numerous cryptocurrency brands, and this is where the opportunity is.

Yours, Y'alls, and Steemit are a few platforms that regularly hire content producers in the cryptocurrency industry.

15. Pay With Crypto

Incorporate cryptocurrency as one of your payment methods. If you're a merchant, you stand a chance of earning handsomely from accepting crypto payments. Statistics show that some cryptos have risen in market value within a day by 1000s in percentage increase, very few investments make it to 100% in years. All you need to do is to identify the best channel for accepting crypto payments; here are a few to get you started:

- CoinBank
- BitPay
- CoinGate
- SpectroCoin.

CONCLUSION

One of the biggest obstacles for investors when it comes to cryptocurrencies is not falling victim to the hype. Digital currencies have become increasingly popular among institutional and ordinary investors alike. Analysts have also kept reminding investors of the volatility and unpredictable nature of cryptocurrencies.

Before investing in cryptocurrencies, you should probably ask yourself why you're doing it, which is perhaps the most important question to ask. Numerous investing options exist, many of which provide more stability and lower risk than virtual currency.

Are you just curious since cryptocurrencies are so popular right now? Or is there a more compelling justification for investing in a particular digital token or tokens? Exploring the cryptocurrency area may make more sense for certain investors than for others, but different investors have different personal investment goals.

Before making an investment, investors must gain a basic understanding of how the world of digital currencies operates.

CONCLUSION

This is especially important for those who are new to the concept. Spend some time getting to know the various currencies on offer. It's important to go beyond the largest names, like Bitcoin, Ether, and Ripple, given the hundreds of different coins and tokens that are accessible.

It's also crucial to learn about blockchain technology to understand how this area of the bitcoin world functions.

It may be difficult for you to understand some parts of blockchain technology if you don't have a background in computer science or coding. There are numerous introductory texts on blockchain technology that are written in plain language.

If you've chosen a cryptocurrency (or cryptocurrencies) to invest in, research how it (they) uses blockchain technology and whether they provide any advances that set them apart from the competition. You'll be better able to assess whether a possible investment opportunity is worthwhile if you have a deeper understanding of cryptocurrencies and blockchain technology.

Because the digital currency industry is so popular, things frequently change and advance swiftly. The fact that a large and vibrant community of fans and investors in digital currencies is constantly interacting is one factor. Reddit has emerged as a key location. There are other additional internet forums with ongoing conversations as well.

However, a digital currency's specifics are more significant than word of mouth. Consider spending some time locating the project's white paper before making an investment. Every cryptocurrency project needs to have one, and if it doesn't, that should be taken as a warning sign.

Read the white paper carefully; it should have all the infor-

CONCLUSION

mation you need to know about the project's developers' goals, including a timeline, a broad overview, and specifics about the project. The absence of statistics and specific project information in the white paper is typically viewed negatively.

You have probably gained an understanding of the cryptocurrency market after thorough research, and you may have chosen one or more projects to invest in. The next step is to time your investment. The field of digital currencies is notorious for its rapid movement and significant volatility.

On the one hand, investing in a hot new currency before it soars in value and popularity can encourage investors to act similarly rapidly. However, if you wait to act until you've carefully studied the market, you'll have a better chance of finding success. The price of cryptocurrencies typically follows certain trends. Among digital currencies, Bitcoin frequently sets the standard since others prefer to follow its general direction. The cryptocurrency community can be rocked by news of an exchange hack, fraud, or price manipulation, so it's crucial to keep an eye on what's happening in the industry more generally.

Last but not least, keep in mind that digital currencies are very speculative. For every bitcoin millionaire who appeared out of nowhere, many other investors have lost money after investing in virtual tokens. Putting money into this market is a risk. Before making an investment, do your research to offer yourself the best chance of success.

BIBLIOGRAPHY

Abrol, A. (2022, March 24). *Complete Guide to Cryptocurrency Trading for Beginners*. Blockchain Council. https://www.blockchain-council.org/cryptocurrency/complete-guide-to-cryptocurrency-trading-for-beginners/

Arora, S. (2022, July 19). *What Is Cryptocurrency: Types, Benefits, History and More.* Simplilearn.Com. https://www.simplilearn.com/tutorials/blockchain-tutorial/what-is-cryptocurrency

Balaban, D. (2017, November 17). *How to Secure Your Cryptocurrency Wallet: 16 Simple Tips for Beginners*. Bitcoinist.Com. https://bitcoinist.com/secure-cryptocurrency-wallet-16-simple-tips-beginners/amp/

The Basics about Cryptocurrency | CTS. (2020). CTS. https://www.oswego.edu/cts/basics-about-cryptocurrency#:%7E:text=A%20cryptocurrency%20is%20a%20digital,you%20need%20a%20cryptocurrency%20wallet.

Beware of Cryptocurrency Scams. (2022, February 8). Investopedia. https://www.investopedia.com/articles/forex/042315/beware-these-five-bitcoin-scams.asp

C. (2022a, July 25). *What Is a DEX (Decentralized Exchange)? | Chainlink.* Chainlink Blog. https://blog.chain.link/dex-decentralized-exchange/

(c) Copyright skillsyouneed.com 2011–2022. (2021). *A Beginner's Guide to Trading Crypto | SkillsYouNeed.* Skills You Need. https://www.skillsyouneed.com/rhubarb/beginners-guide-crypto.html

Cointelegraph. (2022, January 18). *Crypto trading basics: A beginner's guide to cryptocurrency order types.* https://cointelegraph.com/trading-for-beginners/crypto-trading-basics-a-beginners-guide-to-cryptocurrency-order-types/amp

Corporate Finance Institute. (2022, May 6). *Cryptocurrency Exchanges.* https://corporatefinanceinstitute.com/resources/knowledge/other/cryptocurrency-exchanges/

Cryptocurrency Market Size, Growth & Trends | Forecast [2028]. (2021). Fortune Business. https://www.fortunebusinessinsights.com/amp/industry-reports/cryptocurrency-market-100149

Decentralised finance: Understanding the benefits, risks and challenges of DeFi.

BIBLIOGRAPHY

(2022, March 23). Vistra. https://www.vistra.com/insights/decentralised-finance-understanding-benefits-risks-and-challenges-defi?amp

Fang, F. (2022, February 7). *Cryptocurrency trading: a comprehensive survey - Financial Innovation*. SpringerOpen. https://jfin-swufe.springeropen.com/articles/10.1186/s40854-021-00321-6

Freeman, J. B. (2022, January 26). *Overview of the Most Common Cryptocurrencies | Blockchain Technology*. Freeman Law. https://freemanlaw.com/overview-of-the-most-common-cryptocurrencies/

H. (2022b, July 12). *What is decentralized finance (DeFi)?* Hedera. https://hedera.com/learning/decentralized-finance/what-is-decentralized-finance

Levy, A. (2022, June 27). *8 Benefits of Cryptocurrency*. The Motley Fool. https://www.fool.com/investing/stock-market/market-sectors/financials/cryptocurrency-stocks/benefits-of-cryptocurrency/

Lisafi, S. (2022, January 19). *How to Trade Crypto Responsibly*. TatLearn. https://blog.tatcoin.com/trading-crypto-responsibly/

Marr, B. (2021, December 10). *A Short History Of Bitcoin And Crypto Currency Everyone Should Read*. Forbes. https://www.forbes.com/sites/bernardmarr/2017/12/06/a-short-history-of-bitcoin-and-crypto-currency-everyone-should-read/?sh=36aa28e13f27

Mazer, J. (2017, August 24). *Demystifying cryptocurrencies, blockchain, and ICOs*. Toptal Finance Blog. https://www.toptal.com/finance/market-research-analysts/cryptocurrency-market

McNamara, R. (2022, August 4). *How to Trade Cryptocurrency: A Beginners Guide •*. Benzinga. https://www.benzinga.com/how-to-trade-cryptocurrency

Mediawire. (2022, March 12). *Best Crypto Wallet 2022 - Compare 5 Bitcoin Wallet Accounts*. Economic Times. https://m.economictimes.com/industry/banking/finance/best-crypto-wallet-2022-compare-5-bitcoin-wallet-accounts/amp_articleshow/88995218.cms

NI Business Info. (2021). *Advantages and disadvantages of using cryptocurrency | nibusinessinfo.co.uk*. https://www.nibusinessinfo.co.uk/content/advantages-and-disadvantages-using-cryptocurrency

Responsible trading with cryptocurrency. (2021). LogOut. https://www.logout.org/en/blog/responsible-trading-with-cryptocurrency/

Rossolillo, N. (2022, July 5). *What Is a Blockchain Wallet?* The Motley Fool. https://www.fool.com/investing/stock-market/market-sectors/financials/blockchain-stocks/blockchain-wallet/

Rottgen, R. C. F. (2018, January 11). *Investing in Cryptocurrencies: The Ulti-

BIBLIOGRAPHY

mate Guide. Toptal Finance Blog. https://www.toptal.com/finance/fintech/investing-in-cryptocurrencies

S., A. (2022, July 20). *Best Cryptocurrency Wallet*. BitDegree.Org Crypto Exchanges. https://www.bitdegree.org/crypto/amp/best-cryptocurrency-wallet

Store, E. (2021, September 23). *Learn How to Create Wealth Through Cryptocurrency*. Entrepreneur. https://www.entrepreneur.com/article/387408

Sutevski, D. (2022, March 17). *5 Undeniable Advantages of Using a Crypto Wallet for Trading*. Entrepreneurs Box. https://www.entrepreneurshipinabox.com/27934/5-undeniable-advantages-of-using-a-crypto-wallet-for-trading/?amp=1

T. (2021, September 6). *7 Essential Steps to Keep Your Crypto Wallet Secure*. Trust Wallet. https://community.trustwallet.com/t/7-essential-steps-to-keep-your-crypto-wallet-secure/35756

Thompson, B. (2022, August 4). *10 BEST Crypto Wallet Apps (Aug 2022)*. Guru99. https://www.guru99.com/best-bitcoin-cryptocurrency-wallets.html

Weston, G. (2022, July 14). *5 Tips You Must Check Before Choosing the Best Crypto Wallet*. 101 Blockchains. https://101blockchains.com/best-crypto-wallet/

ABOUT THE AUTHOR

Bogdan Ivanov is a Ukrainian-born author and publisher now living in Germany who has been in love with books from a very young age. His passion for literature has fueled his life-long dream to publish books that will inspire, educate, and entertain people worldwide.

With diverse interests, Bogdan enjoys writing about various topics, such as personal development, doomsday prepping, psychology, finances, entrepreneurship, and much more.

He doesn't like to pigeonhole himself to only one topic, which is why he writes about whatever interests him at the moment, so don't be surprised to see one day a couple of fiction books among all the different non-fiction books he has authored. Bogdan's books are a testament to his curious nature and commitment to sharing his knowledge with others.

His unique perspective and writing style make his books a must-read for anyone looking to expand their understanding of the world around them and of themselves.